The
Healthy
Jewish
Kitchen

The
Healthy
Jewish
Kitchen

Fresh, Contemporary Recipes for Every Occasion

Paula Shoyer

STERLING EPICURE
New York

STERLING EPICURE
New York

An Imprint of Sterling Publishing Co., Inc.
1166 Avenue of the Americas
New York, NY 10036

ISBN 978-1-4549-2290-2

Library of Congress Cataloging-in-Publication Data

Names: Shoyer, Paula, author.
Title: The healthy Jewish kitchen : fresh, contemporary recipes for every
  occasion / Paula Shoyer, author of The New Passover Menu and The Holiday
  Kosher Baker.
Description: New York : Sterling Epicure, [2017] | Includes bibliographical
  references and index.
Identifiers: LCCN 2017007609 | ISBN 9781454922902 (book / hc-plc with jacket
  : alk. paper)
Subjects: LCSH: Jewish cooking. | LCGFT: Cookbooks.
Classification: LCC TX724 .S5328 2017 | DDC 641.5/676--dc23 LC record available at
https://lccn.loc.gov/2017007609

Distributed in Canada by Sterling Publishing Co., Inc.
c/o Canadian Manda Group, 664 Annette Street
Toronto, Ontario, Canada M6S 2C8
Distributed in the United Kingdom by GMC Distribution Services
Castle Place, 166 High Street, Lewes, East Sussex, England BN7 1XU
Distributed in Australia by NewSouth Books
45 Beach Street, Coogee, NSW 2034, Australia

For information about custom editions, special sales, and premium and corporate purchases,
please contact Sterling Special Sales at 800-805-5489 or specialsales@sterlingpublishing.com.

Manufactured in China

2 4 6 8 10 9 7 5 3 1

sterlingpublishing.com

Design by Shannon Nicole Plunkett

Principal photography by Bill Milne. Stock photography by iStockphoto.com:
© 5second: 93; © Natasha Breen: 109; © Maryna Laroshenko: 17; © Margouillat photos: 66;
© Merinka: 49; © Mizina: 87; © a_namenko: 29; © Karina Urmantseva: 71, 81

Contents

A *Healing* Project

This is a cookbook about wellness. Writing *The Healthy Jewish Kitchen* was a gift to me from my publisher, and now these recipes are my gift to you.

Sterling Epicure came to me in December 2015 and asked if I would write a healthy kosher food cookbook. It was only one month after my mother, Toby Marcus, *zichrona, l'vracha* (may her memory be a blessing), passed away from cancer. She was diagnosed in August and was gone twelve weeks later. In December, looking ahead to 2016, I knew that I needed something to do, but I wasn't sure what. It is hard to make decisions when you are mourning and tired all the time. All I knew for sure was that standing still was not an option. I needed a new challenge. So I chose the one handed to me. After three cookbooks, writing cookbooks is something I know how to do, and that I enjoy, so I said yes.

The healthy angle was particularly fortuitous. Shiva in the New York area left me bloated. Grieving for months meant bad weeks and worse ones. Bad weeks meant more naps and eating a lot of popcorn. Really bad weeks meant getting into my twins' stash of Ben and Jerry's ice cream. So when this project came along, I knew that it was time for me to eat better. We all need to.

Writing this book brought me back to life. As the months went by and I created more and more recipes that I was really excited about, I found that I felt lighter both physically and emotionally. I actually lost weight writing this book and knew I was onto something.

Most Jewish cookbooks still have too many recipes with processed ingredients, not enough whole grains, too much salt and fat, and too much sugar, even in savory dishes. My goal was to create recipes that use only natural ingredients. I banished margarine, frozen puff pastry, soup stocks and powders, and most jarred sauces (though I gave Dijon mustard a pardon). I gave up frying and created baked goods with as much whole grain flour as I could. I made recipes gluten-free where possible. I reduced sugar and salt.

These recipes include Jewish classics made healthier and updated for the modern table, and both American and international recipes that reflect food trends beyond the Jewish culinary world. This book has food you recognize, because you still want to feel connected to your ancestors' kitchens, but I made the dishes more nutritious and, often, easier to prepare.

This book is a way for you to *start* eating better. I am not standing here preaching—I go to Paris and Israel and eat my way through their best restaurants and bakeries. Good nutrition is about balance and finding a way to introduce into your diet more and more healthful food as often as possible.

I learned firsthand that life is unpredictable: Right before this book went to press, I lost my father, as well. There is no guarantee that eating better will help you live longer. All I know is that now I want to feel good and have energy for the people I love. I am simply offering you a subtle shift toward better health without giving up your favorite foods. The key to better health is homemade and natural food. This is your guidebook.

—Paula

A Healthier Pantry

I am not a nutritionist, although I did consult with a few of them while writing this book. I listened to their suggestions and learned from them, but I was reluctant to send my audience to multiple markets to find ingredients they might never have heard of. I want people to actually make these recipes, not make their lives difficult.

Below was my thinking in using certain ingredients for this book:

SWEETENERS

I was determined not to use anything unnatural or that tasted unnatural, so I avoided all sugar substitutes. Instead, my goal was to use less than 1 cup of sugar per recipe and use honey where possible. Most of the dessert recipes have less than ½ cup sugar, but a few, try as I might, wouldn't work any other way because of the other healthier ingredients in them.

SALT

High salt intake can increase blood pressure and put you at risk for heart attack and stroke. However, salt is an essential nutrient. Kosher food, especially in restaurants, in notoriously oversalted.

If there was one consistent complaint from my team of recipe testers, it was that the recipes all needed more salt. I was definitely conservative in adding salt. I teach teens never to add salt to a finished dish before they taste it; you should do the same. The recipes have a minimum amount of salt, and you can always add more. I found that adding just a pinch of kosher salt to dishes just before serving pumped up flavor, while using less salt overall.

Do your best to add only the amount of salt that is absolutely necessary.

OIL

There are so many different kinds of oil, and once you start using any of the oils listed below, you will be eating better than if you were still using vegetable oil, corn oil, or margarine. Each of the oils has benefits, and the best move for your overall health is to use a variety in your cooking. For this book I did not use any margarine, even the brands that are supposed to be better for your health. There are better fat choices to use that taste better.

Avocado oil: High in vitamin E, avocado oil is flavorful, especially in salads, although it is expensive.

Canola oil: Packed with omega-3s, this oil works well at high cooking temperatures. Many people avoid canola oil, however, because in the United States, most canola oil is made with genetically modified organisms (GMOs). I personally do not have a problem with that.

Coconut (oil and spread): When using these, add other flavors, such as vanilla, so that the coconut taste does not overpower the recipe, unless of course you want it to taste like coconut.

Olive oil: Olive oil lowers bad cholesterol, but avoid using it to cook food at very high temperatures, as it will burn and the health benefits of the oil will be diminished.

Sunflower oil and safflower oil: Both have a mild taste and are good for heart health.

FLOUR

We live during a time in history when the variety of flours available is truly staggering, and they have made baked goods more accessible to people on special diets. Try recipes with types of flours that are new to you and see how you feel.

White all-purpose: The nutrition community claims that white flour is evil because about 93 percent of the fiber, plus a quarter of the protein in the original wheat kernel, is removed during processing. Although the resulting flour is then fortified with vitamins, white flour is still blamed for sugar highs, energy lows, and weight gain. When I want to increase the nutritional content of a dessert, I substitute 25 percent of the white flour with another, healthier flour first. Then, after I've seen the results, I can see if it's possible to substitute even more flour, as well as make other changes, such as adding additional moisture to the recipe. I use unbleached flour in my baking, to avoid the chemicals used in the bleaching process, but these recipes also work with bleached flour.

White whole-wheat: Milled from the hard, white wheat berry. The bran is lighter and sweeter than in the usual wheat berry. White whole-wheat is sometimes considered to be albino wheat. The flour has the same nutritional value as whole-wheat flour. Sometimes it makes baked goods too dry, and I find that I cannot use it alone.

Whole-wheat: I use fine rather than stone-ground whole-wheat flour.

Spelt: Spelt has fewer calories than whole-wheat flour, is higher in protein, and is easier to digest. The use of spelt goes back to the Bronze Age, and it is even mentioned in the Bible.

Almond: I use this flour a lot in my gluten-free baking and often combine it with potato starch to hold dough and batters together. I use a coffee grinder to grind whole nuts, as it is cheaper than buying almond flour and tastes fresher. Almond flour is my go-to flour substitute for Passover baking.

GRAINS

In this book I use brown rice more than white rice, but I also present a new way to prepare white rice that may be lower in calories and higher in nutrition than conventional methods. (See page 102.) In addition, I have recipes that use quinoa and kasha instead of rice, and the only pasta I use is made from whole wheat. I have found that my children cannot tell that I use whole-wheat pasta rather than their beloved white pasta in baked dishes.

MILK SUBSTITUTES

I have long used soy and almond milk in my baking, and now I use coconut milk in many recipes with great results. I have yet to make a dessert recipe in which a particular milk substitute rendered an inferior result.

FAVORITE TOOLS

Scale: When I was in French culinary school, we weighed everything, including eggs. You want a scale for many reasons—to know the weight of everything from chocolate to vegetables for more accurate cooking and baking, and to divide challah dough so your strands are even (use the metric measurement for that). In the absence of weighing, you need to measure precisely. For baking, that means scooping, shaking, and leveling dry ingredients and looking at measured liquids at eye level.

Tongs: They're the best tool for turning chicken and meat or for stirring large amounts of onions or vegetables in a tall pot. Get the silicone-tipped ones.

Box grater: This tool reminds me of my mother and grandmother, who always grated everything by hand—and using it saves you from having to clean the food processor. Recipes in this book will indicate whether to use the small or large holes of the box grater.

Microplane zester: This is a favorite tool, as I use zest in many recipes. It can also be used for grating cheese and fresh ginger. (Buy separate ones for milk and meat.)

Salad spinner: I hate wet lettuce and use a lot of fresh herbs in my recipes. The spinner helps get everything as dry as possible.

Ruler: Many dessert recipes instruct bakers to roll out dough to a certain size or to use a certain size pan. I'm good at that, simply by eyeballing things, but if you don't have that superpower, a ruler makes sure you get it right. Hide it from the kids or you'll never see it again.

Electric citrus juicer: I first bought one when I made lemon tarts in Geneva, Switzerland, as a caterer. The juicer gets more juice out of your citrus than juicing by hand. You can also use a manual juicer.

Food processor: There is a lot of chopping involved in this book. Be nice to your hands and use the processor sometimes.

Immersion blender: A life-changing invention. I couldn't live without this tool, especially for soups.

Onion goggles: A favorite new toy—I mean, tool—that really prevents you from tearing up while chopping onions.

Small liquid measuring cups: These are glass or plastic, with a lip to aid pouring, and usually hold about 4 tablespoons. They are so much easier to use, without spilling, than measuring liquids with spoons.

• How to Use This Book •

Recipes in this book are labeled if they are Dairy, Meat, Parve, Vegan, Vegetarian, or Gluten-free. The Passover label indicates that the recipe is appropriate for Passover or can be adjusted easily to make it so, though I am using the Ashkenazi standard. Other gluten-free recipes with rice or legumes, but without any of the other prohibited grains, may be eaten by Sephardic Jews on Passover.

• What the Labels Mean •

Dairy: Recipes with milk, cheese, butter, yogurt or other dairy products. You can substitute for many recipes as follows to make them nondairy:
- **MILK:** Soy, almond, rice, hemp
- **CHEESE:** Dairy-free cheeses, available in many stores, usually made from soy
- **BUTTER:** Coconut oil (chill or freeze for baked goods), dairy-free margarine
- **YOGURT:** Coconut-based yogurt

Meat: Recipes with different cuts for beef, veal, lamb, chicken

Parve: Recipes that are neither meat nor dairy and can be served with either meat or dairy meals. Eggs and fish are considered parve.

Vegan: recipes without eggs, honey, or dairy

Vegetarian: recipes without meat or fish and might contain dairy or eggs

Gluten-free: recipes without wheat (all species), barley, rye, oats (that have not been cross-contaminated)

Passover: recipes that are kosher for Passover as is, or that can easily be adapted for Passover, following Ashkenazi rules (no corn, rice, legumes)

EQUIPMENT

Every recipe has a list of equipment needed to help streamline your meal preparation, but the items are flexible. For example, if you have a 9-inch pan and the recipe calls for an 8-inch pan, you can use the pan you have, just watch the dish cooking or baking because you might need to adjust the cooking time.

TIP BOXES

Tip boxes throughout the book contain useful techniques and information also relevant to recipes elsewhere.

Most Important Tip

Every oven is different, and some run hotter or colder than others. The recipes in this book were tested on two different brands of ovens in my kitchen, then in the ovens of several recipe testers, so that I could give you the most accurate baking times. But the first time you make any recipe in this book, or really any recipe, shave 10 minutes off the baking time if the recipe calls for baking for 1 hour, shave 5 minutes off 30–60 minutes, and shave 2 minutes off 12–15 minute baking times. Check for doneness and add more time as needed; you can always add time, but you cannot take it away. More people overbake their recipes than underbake them.

Meal Planning

Variety is the key to a delicious, nutritious meal, and the best way to convince your people to go on a healthier eating journey with you. Even my twin teenage boys discovered new foods they loved during the development of this book, and they no longer make faces when presented with a whole-grain dessert. They and their friends love to eat at our home because no meal is ever boring.

First, I make sure every dinner plate has a variety of colors and textures. Next, I make sure that we eat both raw and cooked vegetables at every meal. Not every child has to love every dish on the table, but as long as there is at least one thing each kid will eat, a meal works. There are no separate meals for different family members.

I remember being at a friend's home at the end of the day while her nanny was cooking. I asked why she was preparing only a small amount—weren't my friend and her husband eating with their children? She said that she would cook a separate meal later for her husband and herself. I thought she was kidding. Children are people and should just eat good food. Kid food is simply a way of dumbing down food and nutrition. Once their first two teeth came in, our children have always eaten the same meal as my husband and I.

No one loves every vegetable or every preparation of all vegetables. Figure out what works for your crew, like French daycare teachers do when introducing new foods to 18-month-old children. They try shredded raw carrots first and see if the students eat them. They might try cooked carrots next and carrot purée after that. They believe that there must be a way to get a child who says he doesn't like carrots to eat them. Usually they find a method that appeals. American parents tend to give up when their kids try something once and claim they hate it. Keep introducing healthy foods in different forms until you get a hit. And what your child hates at age 2 might be her favorite food at age 5. At my twins' seventeen-year-old check-up, our pediatrician turned to me with amazement and asked how I produced four good eaters; he had never seen that before in his practice. Another reason to work hard to introduce children to a wide variety is because if they develop allergies or other ailments as they grow up, they will still have many foods they like to eat.

Healthy eating requires planning and time management. Start soaking beans or rice before you go to sleep. Make sure you have all the ingredients you need several hours before you start cooking. See what takes the longest. If you have a free 15 minutes in the middle of the day, make a part of the meal—spread out the parts of a dish. My mother worked full time, so she always made Shabbat dinner on Thursday night. I almost never bake challah on Friday; challahs are done by Wednesday and are then frozen. I make desserts and soups on Thursday to make my Fridays less stressful. Not every dish should be time-consuming—create a menu that combines easy and fancy dishes. Have some soups and desserts in the freezer and build from there.

Menu Suggestions

SHABBAT LUNCH

Israeli Herb and Almond Salad

Chopped Salad with Lemon and Sumac Dressing

Asian Sweet Potato Salad

Winter Red Salad

Apple, Squash, and Brussels Sprout Salad

Crudités with Red Pepper Tahini

Feijoada: Brazilian Cholent
with Collard Greens and Farofa

Grilled Steak with Everything Marinade

Arroz con Pollo with Brown Rice and Salsa Verde

Indian Barbecued Chicken

Kasha Mujadarra

Sri Lankan Rice with Dried Fruits and Nuts

Eggplant with Capers and Mint

Charred Cauliflower with Orange Vinaigrette

Grilled Corn with Cilantro Pesto

Whole-Wheat Onion Challah

Sourdough Challah

THANKSGIVING DINNER

Apple, Squash, and Brussels Sprout Salad

Ribollita

Sage and Shallot Roasted Turkey
with Whole-Wheat Stuffing

Grilled Corn with Cilantro Pesto

Tzimmis Purée

Fruit Galette with a Chocolate Crust

Rosemary Focaccia

ROSH HASHANAH

Tuscan Farro Soup

Brisket Bourguignon

Whole Roasted Chicken with Quinoa
and Pine Nut Stuffing

Sri Lankan Rice with Dried Fruits and Nuts

Tzimmis Purée

Roasted Broccoli with Mustard
and Za'atar Drizzle

Caramelized Apple Strudel

Israeli Chocolate Rugelach

Root Vegetable and Apple Cake

Blueberry Honey Cake Scones

CHANUKAH

Potato and Scallion Latkes with Pickled Applesauce

PURIM

Pumpkin Hamantaschen

PASSOVER

Israeli Herb Salad

Chopped Salad with Lemon Sumac Dressing

Winter Red Salad

Apple, Squash, and Brussels Sprout Salad

Mango Coleslaw

Watermelon, Peach, and Mint Gazpacho

Bouillabaisse

Modern Borscht: Beet and Parsnip Purée

Tzatziki Soup

French Onion Soup with Flanken

Baked Schnitzel with Nut Crust

Brisket Bourguignon

Indian Barbecued Chicken

Whole Roasted Chicken with Quinoa
and Pine Nut Stuffing

Coq au Vin Blanc

Red Quinoa Meatballs with Spaghetti Squash

Dry-Rubbed Roasted Salmon

Spiced Fish with Cauliflower Purée and
Red Pepper Tomato Relish

Quinoa with Mushrooms and Kale

Potato and Scallion Latkes with
Pickled Applesauce

Brussels Sprout Crumbs

Tzimmis Purée

Eggplant with Capers and Mint

Chocolate Quinoa Cake

SHAVUOT

Tzatziki Soup

Watermelon, Peach, and Mint Gazpacho

Bouillabaisse

Cheese-Filled Buckwheat Blintzes

Fish Tacos with Cilantro Lime Rice

Dry-Rubbed Roasted Salmon

Pasta Siciliana

Mini Cheesecakes with Oat and Brown Sugar Crust
and Strawberry Purée

BBQ

Watermelon, Peach, and Mint Gazpacho

Charred Cauliflower with Orange Vinaigrette

Asian Sweet Potato Salad

Mango Coleslaw

Grilled Steak with Everything Marinade

Indian Barbecued Chicken

Japanese Lamb Chops

Peas and Carrots Reinvented:
Grilled Whole Carrots with English Pea Dip

Grilled Corn with Cilantro Pesto

Fruit Cobbler with Chickpea and
Almond Topping

Appetizers
and
Salads

ISRAELI HERB AND ALMOND SALAD

Parve, Gluten-free, Vegan, Passover • Serves 6

This versatile salad, which appears in some version on every Israeli hotel breakfast buffet, can be served with yogurt or eggs for breakfast and alongside any grilled fish, chicken, or steak dish for lunch or dinner. I've even served this salad with gefilte fish. To make a meal of the salad, you can add feta, chickpeas (but not on Passover), or tuna. Always use the freshest herbs you can find, and wash and dry them very well.

PREP TIME: 20 minutes • COOK TIME: 15 minutes to toast almonds • ADVANCE PREP: May be made 3 days in advance • EQUIPMENT: Cutting board, chef's knife, salad spinner, citrus juicer, garlic press, jelly roll pan or cookie sheet, food processor, measuring cups and spoons, paper towels, large bowl, small bowl, whisk, tongs

⅓ cup (40g) slivered almonds

2 large bunches Italian parsley, thick stems removed

1 large bunch dill, stems removed

1 cup (50g) mint leaves

4 scallions, ends trimmed, thinly sliced

¼ cup (60ml) extra virgin olive oil

Juice of 1 lemon (about 3½ tablespoons)

1 clove garlic, crushed

¼ teaspoon kosher salt

¼ teaspoon black pepper, or more to taste

1 pint (300g) cherry tomatoes, halved if small or quartered if large

• Preheat oven to 325°F (160°C). Place the almonds on a cookie sheet and toast for 12 to 15 minutes, or until light golden and fragrant. Shake the pan once during baking. Set aside and let cool.

• Wash the herbs in batches in a salad spinner and dry very well. Chop the parsley (about 2½ cups [125g]), dill (about 2 cups [100g]), and mint by hand or in a food processor into small, but not tiny, pieces. Even after the herbs are chopped, I grab more paper towels to press into them to absorb more moisture. Place with the scallions in a large bowl.

• In a small bowl, place the olive oil, lemon juice, garlic, salt, and pepper and whisk well. Add to the herbs and toss to coat. Add the tomatoes and mix. Taste and add more salt and pepper if needed. Add the almonds right before serving and toss well.

Washing and Drying Fresh Herbs

Fill a salad spinner or bowl with cold water. Submerge the herbs and move them around to loosen any dirt. Lift the strainer part of the spinner out of the water. If the water is clean, the herbs are clean. If the water is dirty, dump the water out, rinse the bowl, refill it, and repeat until the water is clean. Spin to get as much water as possible off the herbs, and then use paper towels to dry them even more.

Storing Fresh Herbs

Rosemary, sage, and thyme should be wrapped in a damp paper towel and stored in a plastic bag in the fridge. Herbs such as parsley, dill, mint, tarragon, and cilantro should be stored in the fridge with the stems placed in a jar with water, like a bouquet of flowers, and then covered loosely with a plastic bag. Basil should be stored at room temperature in water away from direct sunlight.

CHOPPED SALAD WITH LEMON AND SUMAC DRESSING

Dairy (if using cheese), Parve and Vegan (if not using cheese), Gluten-free, Passover • Serves 6 to 8

Anyone who has heard my four secrets to staying fit as a chef will already know that I eat a lot of salad. If you grew up in the era when iceberg lettuce and salads composed of fewer than five ingredients were popular, you'll love this modern chopped salad. There is no wrong way to make a salad—you can add other ingredients to this recipe, such as tuna, hard-boiled eggs, chickpeas, cannellini beans, or any vegetable you like to eat raw.

PREP TIME: 15 minutes • ADVANCE PREP: Dressing may be made 3 days in advance; assemble salad right before serving; best eaten day of preparation • EQUIPMENT: Cutting board, knife, measuring cups and spoons, citrus juicer, garlic press, large bowl, small bowl or glass measuring cup, whisk, tongs

SALAD

2 scallions, ends trimmed, cut into ¼-inch (12-mm) pieces

½ red bell pepper, cut into ¾-inch (2-cm) pieces

8 pitted green olives, halved the long way

½ small red onion, chopped into ¼-inch (6-mm) pieces (about ¼ cup)

½ English cucumber, unpeeled, cut into 1-inch (2.5-cm) pieces

1 endive, halved the long way and sliced

½ fennel bulb, chopped into ½-inch (12-mm) pieces

1 avocado, cut into 1-inch (2.5-cm) cubes

1 cup (20g) baby spinach leaves, roughly chopped

2 cups (40g) arugula leaves, or any type of lettuce, cut into 1 to 1½-inch (2.5- to 4-cm) pieces

1 cup (150g) multicolored cherry tomatoes, halved

½ cup (75g) cubed feta cheese, cut into ¾- to 1-inch (2-cm to 2.5-cm) cubes (optional)

DRESSING

Juice of ½ lemon, or more to taste

4 tablespoons extra virgin olive oil

½ teaspoon sumac

1 clove garlic, crushed

¼ teaspoon salt

¼ teaspoon black pepper

Pinch kosher salt, if needed after tasting

• To make the salad, put the scallions, bell peppers, olives, red onions, cucumbers, endive, fennel, avocadoes, spinach, arugula, and cherry tomatoes into a large bowl.

• To make the dressing, place the lemon juice, olive oil, sumac, garlic, salt, and pepper in a small bowl or glass measuring cup and whisk well. Pour the dressing over the vegetables and toss. Taste the salad. Sprinkle kosher salt on top, if needed, and toss before serving.

• Scatter feta cheese on top, if using.

Sumac

Sumac is a flowering plant grown in Africa, North America, and East Asia that produces red berries that are dried and ground. In Middle Eastern cooking it is used as a garnish to salads, while Iranians add it to meat kebabs and rice. Throughout history sumac has also been used as medicine or as a dye.

CRUDITÉS WITH RED PEPPER TAHINI

Parve, Gluten-free, Vegan • Serves 6, or more as a nosh before dinner

This red pepper tahini can be served with anything—schnitzel, grilled meat, or fish—or use it as a dip for bread.

PREP TIME: 10 minutes; 15 minutes to let peppers cool • COOK TIME: 10 to 15 minutes to roast peppers • ADVANCE PREP: Tahini may be made 4 days in advance • EQUIPMENT: Cutting board, knife, measuring cups and spoons, citrus juicer, jelly roll pan or cookie sheet, medium bowl, plastic wrap, food processor, silicone spatula, small bowl

2 red bell peppers, halved, seeds and white veins removed

1 tablespoon extra virgin olive oil, plus more for drizzling on peppers

⅛ teaspoon smoked paprika

¼ cup (60ml) tahini

1 teaspoon fresh lemon juice

⅛ teaspoon salt

1½ cups (225g) baby carrots

4 stalks celery, cut into sticks

1 yellow or orange bell pepper, cut into 1-inch (2.5-cm) strips, seeds and white veins removed

3 Persian cucumbers, cut into sticks

• Preheat oven to broil. Place the red bell peppers on a cookie sheet, drizzle with the olive oil, and rub to coat. Roast for 10 to 15 minutes, or until the peppers are blackened. Remove the peppers from the oven and place into a bowl. Cover the bowl with plastic wrap and let sit for 15 minutes, or until the peppers are cool and you have time to peel them.

• Peel off the blackened skin and discard it. Place the broiled peppers in a food processor. Add the olive oil, smoked paprika, tahini, lemon juice, and salt, and process until puréed. Serve in a bowl next to the vegetables.

MANGO COLESLAW

Parve, Gluten-free, Vegan, Passover • Serves 8

This recipe uses three types of cabbage, but you can also substitute with arugula, slivered spinach leaves, or sliced fennel, or add half a shredded carrot for more color, if you like. The dressing can be used on any salad. Serve this coleslaw with Fish Tacos with Cilantro Lime Rice on page 68, the Grilled Steak with Everything Marinade on page 60, or the Baked Schnitzel with Nut Crust on page 55.

PREP TIME: 10 minutes • ADVANCE PREP: Dressing may be made 2 days in advance; salad may be made 1 day in advance • EQUIPMENT: Vegetable peeler, cutting board, knife, measuring cups and spoons, citrus juicer, food processor, large bowl, tongs to toss the salad

DRESSING

1 large ripe mango, peeled and cut into 1- to 2-inch pieces

2 tablespoons finely chopped red onion

Juice of 1 lime, about 2 to 3 tablespoons

1 teaspoon apple cider vinegar

2 tablespoons avocado, sunflower, or safflower oil

½ cup (20g) loosely packed cilantro leaves

1 teaspoon honey

½ large green chili pepper, such as jalapeño

¼ teaspoon salt

¼ teaspoon black pepper

SALAD

2 cups (200g) shredded red cabbage, about ½ small head

2 cups (200g) shredded green cabbage, about ½ small head

2 cups (200g) shredded Napa cabbage, about 1/3 head

4 scallions, ends trimmed, sliced

• To make the dressing, place the mango, red onions, lime juice, vinegar, oil, cilantro, honey, chili pepper, salt, and black pepper into the bowl of a food processor. Process until puréed; it will be a yellow sauce with green specks.

• To make the salad, in a large bowl, place the shredded cabbages and scallions and toss. Add the mango dressing and mix well.

Chopping Onions

Trim the ends off the onion and cut it in half the long way. Peel off the skin. Place one half, cut side down, on a cutting board, with one end facing toward the tip of your knife. With your knife, cut slices into the onion lengthwise, in the width that you want, but do not slice all the way through the onion; keeping the onion partially intact on one end gives you stability in cutting. Make perpendicular cuts across the long slices all the way until your first cuts end. Turn the small piece of the onion around and then cut slices into that piece. Slice across that slice.

APPLE, SQUASH, AND BRUSSELS SPROUT SALAD

Parve, Gluten-free, Vegan, Passover (substitute for the rice vinegar) • Serves 6

This is a great salad or side dish to serve in the fall—perfect for Thanksgiving dinner or Sukkot lunch.

PREP TIME: 15 minutes • COOK TIME: 30 minutes • ADVANCE PREP: May be made 2 days in advance • EQUIPMENT: Cutting board, knife, measuring cups and spoons, garlic press, jelly roll or roasting pan, silicone spatula, fork, large bowl, small bowl, whisk

1½ pounds (700g) Brussels sprouts, trimmed and halved

3 tablespoons plus 2 teaspoons avocado, sunflower, or safflower oil, divided

3 cups butternut squash, cut into 1-inch (2.5-cm) cubes

3 tablespoons maple syrup

3 cloves garlic, crushed

1 tablespoon rice vinegar

¼ teaspoon allspice

½ teaspoon ground cinnamon

1 tablespoon water

1 red apple, unpeeled, chopped into ¾-inch (2-cm) pieces

¼ teaspoon salt, or more to taste

¼ teaspoon black pepper

• Preheat oven to 400°F (200°C). Place the prepared Brussels sprouts on one side of a jelly roll or roasting pan and toss with 1 tablespoon of oil. Place the butternut squash cubes on the other side of the pan and toss with 2 teaspoons oil. Roast for 30 minutes, or until fork-tender. Let vegetables cool.

• Place the roasted vegetables into a large serving bowl. In a small bowl, whisk together the remaining 2 tablespoons oil and the maple syrup, garlic, rice vinegar, allspice, cinnamon, and water. Pour over the vegetables and toss well. Add the apple pieces and toss again. Add salt and pepper. Serve at room temperature.

Cleaning Brussels Sprouts

You should follow your own rabbinic authority for instructions for cleaning and inspecting Brussels sprouts. I trim off the ends and then remove and discard two layers of outer leaves. I then rinse the sprouts. To be extra careful to avoid bugs, after chopping the sprouts, soak them in water, drain them, and check the water to see if any dirt or bugs are present, and then repeat the process. Dry the sprouts well before proceeding with a recipe.

TUNA POKE

Parve, Gluten-free, Fish • Serves 6

When our family went to Hawaii to celebrate my fiftieth birthday, we pretty much lived on tuna poke (pronounced "POE-kay"), made a variety of ways. Poke is the Hawaiian version of tuna tartare, raw tuna mixed with different spices and sauces. When we were traveling to the town of Volcano on the Big Island, I read about a supermarket that sold poke from the deli counter. Although I was skeptical about buying raw fish from a huge grocery store, I bought two different flavors, along with a bag of taro chips. We ate up the poke immediately, and when we passed the store again, on our departure, we went inside to buy more. Sushi-grade tuna is pricey, so check with your local fish store to find out when they get their tuna, and plan to make this recipe when it is freshest. You can also buy tuna sashimi from a sushi restaurant and use it to make poke.

PREP TIME: 10 minutes • ADVANCE PREP: Must be made and served on the same day • EQUIPMENT: Cutting board, knife, measuring cups and spoons, whisk, silicone spatula, kitchen scissors

1½ pounds (680g) fresh sushi-grade tuna, cut into ¾-inch (2-cm) cubes

⅓ cup (35g) finely chopped red onion

3 tablespoons chopped chives, about ⅓-inch (8-mm) pieces

5 tablespoons tamari soy sauce

3 tablespoons plus 1 teaspoon sesame oil

1 sheet dried seaweed

• Place the tuna into a large bowl. Add the onions, chives, tamari, and sesame oil and mix well. Use kitchen scissors to cut the seaweed into thin, 1-inch (2.5-cm) strips and add them to the bowl. Serve immediately with taro chips, crackers, toasted bread.

Favorite Tools—Kitchen Scissors

I am a huge fan of high-quality kitchen scissors, which you must hide from your school-age children, who will want to use them for arts-and-crafts projects. I use mine to cut whole chickens, short ribs, and other types of meat into pieces, as well as to chop chives, slice basil and other herbs, and cut parchment to fit pans—and the list of uses goes on and on.

ASIAN SWEET POTATO SALAD

Parve, Gluten-free, Vegan • Serves 6 to 8

When I was growing up, deli sandwiches or hot dogs were always served with a creamy, mayonnaise-covered potato salad. My grandmother Sylvia's version had lots of onions and white vinegar, which gave her salad a sharp taste. I wanted to offer up a new potato salad, this time with sweet potatoes and without mayonnaise, but still creamy.

PREP TIME: 10 minutes • COOK TIME: 15 minutes • ADVANCE PREP: May be made 2 days in advance • EQUIPMENT: Vegetable peeler, cutting board, knife, 2-cup (480-ml) glass measuring cup, measuring cups and spoons, medium saucepan, fork, whisk, silicone spatula, medium bowl

2 pounds (1 kg) sweet potatoes, peeled and cut into 3-inch (7.5-cm) chunks

¼ cup (60g) natural, smooth peanut butter

¼ cup (60ml) boiling water

1 tablespoon tamari soy sauce

2 teaspoons sesame oil

1 teaspoon honey

¼ teaspoon rice vinegar

2 tablespoons chopped cilantro

2 pinches cayenne pepper

2 scallions, ends trimmed, sliced

Black sesame seeds (optional)

2 tablespoons chopped roasted peanuts (optional)

• In a medium saucepan, bring 8 cups (2L) water to a boil over medium heat. Add the sweet potato chunks and cook until barely fork-tender, about 15 minutes. Be careful not to overcook. Drain and let cool completely.

• Meanwhile, prepare the dressing. Measure the peanut butter in a 2-cup (500-ml) glass measuring cup. Add the boiling water, and stir or whisk to dissolve the peanut butter in the water. Add the tamari, sesame oil, honey, rice vinegar, cilantro, and cayenne pepper. Whisk well.

• When the sweet potatoes are cool, cut them into 1-inch (2.5-cm) cubes and place them in a medium serving bowl. Add the dressing and mix gently. Sprinkle the scallions and sesame seeds or chopped peanuts on top, if you like, and serve.

WINTER RED SALAD

Parve, Gluten-free, Vegan, Passover • Serves 6

This salad gives a blast of vivid color and crunch to an otherwise not very colorful main course such as simple chicken or fish. Feel free to use precooked beets, which can now be found in most supermarkets.

PREP TIME: 10 minutes • COOK TIME: 45 minutes to roast beets • ADVANCE PREP: Beets may be made 3 days in advance and stored in the fridge; dressing may be made 3 days in advance; salad may be assembled 1 day in advance • EQUIPMENT: Cutting board, knife, measuring cups and spoons, vegetable peeler, Microplane zester, citrus juicer, aluminum foil, jelly roll or roasting pan, whisk, silicone spatula, tongs

SALAD

3 medium red beets, greens trimmed off, unpeeled

2 cups (200g) shredded red cabbage, about half a large head

1 small head radicchio, cut into 1½-inch (4-cm) pieces, about 2½ cups (500g) sliced

½ small red onion, halved and very thinly sliced

2 radishes, peeled into thin slices with a vegetable peeler

½ cup (70g) dried cranberries

¼ cup (40g) pomegranate seeds (optional)

DRESSING

1 teaspoon orange zest (from 1 orange)

1 tablespoon fresh orange juice, from zested orange

1 tablespoon finely chopped shallots (1 small or ½ large bulb)

2 teaspoons balsamic vinegar

1 tablespoon water

1 teaspoon honey

3 tablespoons extra virgin olive oil

¼ teaspoon salt, or more to taste

¼ teaspoon black pepper, or more to taste

• Preheat oven to 400°F (200°C). Rinse, dry, and then wrap each beet in aluminum foil. Place the beets on a jelly roll pan and bake for 45 minutes, or until you can pierce the center with a fork. Remove the beets from the oven and peel them when they are cool enough to handle. May be made 3 days in advance and stored in the fridge.

• To make the dressing, place the orange zest in a medium bowl with the orange juice, shallots, vinegar, water, honey, olive oil, salt, and pepper and whisk well. Dressing may be made 3 days in advance.

• To assemble the salad, place the cabbage, radicchio, red onions, radishes, and cranberries into a large bowl. Cut the beets into 1-inch (2.5-cm) cubes or wedges and add to the bowl. Whisk the dressing and pour over the salad. Toss well. Taste and add salt and pepper if needed, and serve. Sprinkle pomegranate seeds on top, if desired.

CAMBODIAN SPRING ROLLS WITH LIME, CHILI, AND PEANUT DIPPING SAUCE

Parve, Gluten-free, Vegan • Serves 6

In December 2014, my family took a trip to Vietnam and Cambodia. In Siem Riep, Cambodia, we went to the Peace Café, a vegetarian restaurant that came highly recommended. We took a family cooking class in a hut that we climbed up a ladder to enter, and we made these fresh spring rolls. If you like, you can also add leftover salmon or cooked soup chicken (see page 33) to the filling.

PREP TIME: 20 minutes • COOK TIME: 3 minutes • ADVANCE PREP: Sauce may be made 3 days in advance; spring rolls are best served the day they are made • EQUIPMENT: Citrus juicer, measuring cups and spoons, cutting board, knife, vegetable peeler, box grater, small saucepan, whisk, small bowl, pie plate or roasting pan, parchment, plate

DIPPING SAUCE

½ cup (120ml) water

2 tablespoons fresh lime juice

1 tablespoon coconut sugar

¼ to ½ teaspoon dried red pepper flakes, or to taste

2 tablespoons natural, crunchy peanut butter

SPRING ROLLS

12 round rice paper wrappers

12 Bibb lettuce leaves or 6 Romaine lettuce leaves, vein cut out and cut into large pieces

12 large basil leaves

1 cup (50g) mint leaves (2 to 3 leaves per spring roll)

⅔ English cucumber, cut into sticks about 3 inches (7.5cm) long and ½ inch (12mm) wide

2 carrots, peeled and grated on the large holes of a box grater, about 2 cups (220g)

• To make the dipping sauce, place the water, lime juice, coconut sugar, and red pepper flakes into a small saucepan over medium heat. Bring the sauce to a boil and then cook it for 3 minutes over low heat. Remove the saucepan from the heat, whisk in the peanut butter, and transfer the sauce to a small bowl. May be made 3 days in advance.

• To make the spring rolls, have all filling ingredients ready. Fill a pie plate or 9 x 13-inch (23 x 33-cm) pan with about an inch (2.5cm) of water. Place a piece of parchment paper in front of you. Take each rice paper wrapper and dip it into the water, submerging it completely for 20 seconds. Place the softened wrapper on top of the parchment. Place the lettuce leaf just below the middle of the wrapper. Place a basil leaf, 2 to 3 mint leaves, 2 cucumber sticks, and some shredded carrots, about 2½ tablespoons, on top.

• Fold the top of the wrapper up over the filling and squeeze tightly. Roll it over again. Fold the sides of the wrapper toward the middle and then roll it up. Place the roll on a plate. When all the rolls have been made, slice each one in half by cutting it diagonally across the middle.

• Serve the rolls with the dipping sauce.

SYLVIA'S TURKEY STUFFED CABBAGE

Meat, Gluten-free • Serves 6 to 8

I have written stories about my grandma Sylvia Altman in all my cookbooks, because she was the person who first inspired me to bake and challenge myself in the kitchen. Her stuffed cabbage was legendary. She came to Washington, D.C., when she was probably 88 years old, and we cooked it together, with me furiously trying to write down amounts and instructions as she measured with her hands. Grandma's version is made with beef and white rice, and she would use four different saucepans to make the dish. I lightened up both the recipe and the amount of cleanup required. She also used round green cabbage, but I have found that Napa leaves are easier to roll up. This dish tastes better with each passing day.

PREP TIME: 20 minutes • COOK TIME: 3 hours • ADVANCE PREP: May be made 3 days in advance or frozen • EQUIPMENT: Measuring cups and spoons, vegetable peeler, cutting board, knife, can opener, citrus juicer, medium or large saucepan, large colander, large bowl, tongs, paper towels, Dutch oven or other large saucepan, silicone spatula

CABBAGE ROLLS

1 head Napa cabbage, bottom trimmed off

1 medium onion

1 pound (450g) ground turkey, dark meat if possible

⅓ cup (65g) brown rice

1 large egg

¼ cup (60ml) water

½ teaspoon salt

¼ teaspoon black pepper

¼ cup (40g) golden raisins

TOMATO SAUCE

1 tablespoon sunflower, safflower, or other mild oil

2 medium onions

1 large green apple, peeled and cut into ¾-inch (2-cm) cubes

1 28-ounce (795-g) can crushed tomatoes

Juice of 1½ lemons, about 4 tablespoons

¼ cup (55g) light brown sugar

1 tablespoon honey

½ teaspoon salt

½ teaspoon black pepper

• Cut off the end of the cabbage and separate 15 leaves. Bring a medium or large saucepan of water to a boil. Place a colander over a bowl near the saucepan. Cook the leaves, about 5 at a time, for 4 minutes per batch, leaving the water boiling the entire time. Use tongs to lift the cooked leaves out of the saucepan, one at a time, and place in the colander to drain. Try not to tear the leaves. Rinse the cooked leaves under cold water and then place them on paper towels to dry.

• To make the tomato sauce, in a large saucepan or Dutch oven, heat the oil over medium heat. Chop 2 of the onions into small dice, about ½-inch (12-mm) pieces, and add them to a large saucepan or Dutch oven along with the apple cubes. Cook the mixture, stirring it occasionally, until the onions start to soften but not brown, about 10 minutes. Add the crushed tomatoes and then fill the can halfway with water (a little less than 2 cups [480ml]) and add it to the saucepan. Add the lemon juice, brown sugar, and honey and bring to a boil. Add the salt and pepper and simmer, covered.

• To make the filling, finely chop the remaining onion either by hand or in a food processor. Place it in a large bowl. Add the ground turkey, rice, egg, water, salt, and pepper, and mix well with your hands. Scoop

up a handful of the mixture, about 2 to 3 tablespoons for each roll, and place it in the bottom of a cabbage leaf, at the stem. Fan out the cabbage leaf.

• Fold the bottom of the cabbage leaf over the mixture and roll it over again, then fold the sides of the leaf toward the middle to cover the meat, and then roll it up. When all the rolls are ready, place them in the tomato sauce and sprinkle the raisins all around. Cook the rolls, covered over low heat, for 3 hours, carefully stirring the bottom one or twice with a silicone spatula to prevent sticking.

Buffets are Usually the Way to Go

I am a huge fan of serving the main course as a buffet for several reasons. First, I can keep food hotter longer because I can place on the buffet table a baking dish that would be too hot to hold and pass. Second, by not transferring everything into smaller serving dishes to be passed around, I have less cleanup afterward. Third, when bowls and platters are on the table, I will keep adding more food to my plate; if food is on the buffet, I will think twice before getting up to take more, so I eat less. Finally, happy, chatty people pass food very, very slowly, so by the time the serving bowl is passed to you, the food inside it will be cold.

SALMON AND AVOCADO TARTARE

Parve, Gluten-free, Fish, Passover • Serves 8 (⅓-cup servings)

Tartare is the French version of poke, ceviche, and sashimi. I was working on a gefilte fish recipe when I got a call from my friend Chana Kaplan, who runs Friendship Circle at Chabad in Potomac, Maryland. I told her that I was agonizing over a gefilte fish recipe idea that just wasn't panning out. When Chana said that there were enough gefilte fish recipes out there in the world, I mentioned an idea for salmon tartare as a lighter alternative. Chana convinced me to abandon my plan to include a gefilte fish recipe in this book. This tartare is infinitely easier to prepare and can be doubled and tripled for a crowd.

PREP TIME: 10 minutes • ADVANCE PREP: Must be made and served on the same day • EQUIPMENT: Cutting board, knife, Microplane zester, citrus juicer, measuring cups and spoons, kitchen scissors, large bowl, silicone spatula

1 pound (450g) of the freshest salmon or sashimi you can buy

3 scallions, ends trimmed, sliced

1 radish, finely chopped

Zest of ½ lime

1 teaspoon lime juice, from zested lime

1 tablespoon avocado oil

1 ripe avocado, cut into ½-inch (12-mm) cubes

1 basil leaf, cut into ribbons, about 1 tablespoon

1 or 2 tablespoons micro greens, for garnish (optional)

• Slice the salmon into ½-inch (12-mm) cubes. Place them in a large bowl. Add the scallions, radishes, and lime zest and mix. Cover the mixture and refrigerate until just before serving.

• When you're ready to serve the tartare, add the lime juice, avocado oil, avocado cubes, and basil and mix well. Garnish with a sprinkle of micro greens, if you like.

Soups

CREAM OF BROCCOLI SOUP

Gluten-free, Vegan, Passover • Serves 8 to 10

I started making vegetable purée soups back when I was practicing law many years ago. I would cook soups at home, take them into work, and then reheat and eat them at my desk so that I could get right back to work. Soup is definitely the hardest category of recipe writing for me, because I simply never measure anything when I make soup. Most of my vegetable soups are made with whatever I happen to find in the fridge. So feel free to substitute the broccoli in this recipe with 2 pounds (1kg) of any vegetable (or vegetables) you already have, and use this base recipe to clean out your fridge, like I do. See tip box below.

PREP TIME: 8 minutes • COOK TIME: 30 minutes • ADVANCE PREP: May be made 3 days in advance or frozen • EQUIPMENT: Measuring cups and spoons, cutting board, knife, garlic press, can opener, large saucepan or soup pot, silicone spatula, fork, immersion blender or food processor

¼ cup (60ml) extra virgin olive oil

2 medium onions, halved and sliced

2 stalks celery, chopped into ½-inch (12-mm) pieces

1 tablespoon chopped fresh ginger

2 pounds (1kg) broccoli

1 teaspoon ground turmeric

¼ teaspoon plus ⅛ teaspoon white pepper, divided

¼ teaspoon ground coriander

4 cloves garlic, crushed and divided

6 cups (1.4L) water

½ teaspoon salt, divided

1 cup (40g) packed large basil leaves, almost 1 large bunch (reserve some leaves, for garnish)

½ cup (120ml) canned coconut milk

Kosher salt to taste

• Pour the oil into a large saucepan or soup pot over medium heat. Add the onions, celery, and ginger and cook for 10 minutes, stirring occasionally. While the onions are cooking, cut the crowns off the top of the broccoli (the greenest parts), and measure 1½ cups (135g) of crowns. (If you like, reserve a few broccoli florets to garnish the soup before serving.) Set them aside and cut up the remaining broccoli into 2-inch (5-cm) pieces.

• Add the turmeric, ¼ teaspoon white pepper, ground coriander, large pieces of broccoli, 2 cloves crushed garlic, water, and ¼ teaspoon salt, and bring to a boil over medium-high heat. Reduce the heat to low, and cook the mixture for 20 minutes, or until the broccoli is fork-tender. Turn off the heat.

• Add the broccoli crowns, remaining 2 cloves crushed garlic, basil, remaining ¼ teaspoon salt, and remaining ⅛ teaspoon white pepper, then cover and let sit for 10 minutes. Use an immersion blender to purée or use a food processor to blend the mixture in batches, for 3 whole minutes each, until it is very smooth. Add the coconut milk and a little kosher salt to taste and purée for another minute.

Repurposing Vegetables

After sitting shiva for both my parents within a year and a half of each another, I discovered that I could turn any leftover crudite platter or roasted vegetable side into a tasty soup.

RIBOLLITA

Parve, Gluten-free, Vegan • Serves 8 to 10

This Italian classic is usually made with stale bread. I've found that it is really filling, however—a complete meal for lunch—without the bread. If you like, serve the soup with toasted slices of whole-wheat Rosemary Focaccia (page 135) on the side. You can also use curly kale for this recipe, but lacinato is heartier and looks particularly nice in the soup.

PREP TIME: 10 minutes • COOK TIME: 50 minutes • ADVANCE PREP: May be made 3 days in advance or frozen • EQUIPMENT: Measuring cups and spoons, cutting board, knife, vegetable peeler, can opener, large saucepan or soup pot, colander, food processor, fork

2 tablespoons extra virgin olive oil

1 large onion, halved and chopped into ½-inch (12-mm) pieces

2 leeks, light green and white parts only, quartered and sliced

2 carrots, peeled and sliced

2 stalks celery, chopped into ½-inch (12-mm) pieces

2 cloves garlic, roughly chopped

2 15.5-ounce (440-g) cans cannellini beans, divided

7 cups water (1.7L), divided

3 tomatoes, seeds removed, cut into 1-inch (2.5-cm) pieces

1 zucchini, chopped into 1-inch (2.5-cm) pieces

1 cup butternut squash cubes, cut into ¾- to 1-inch (2- to 2.5-cm) cubes

10 leaves lacinato kale (the variety with large bumpy-looking leaves), cut into 1½-inch (4-cm) pieces, about 1½ to 2 cups

Leaves from 6 sprigs fresh thyme

¼ teaspoon kosher salt

¼ teaspoon black pepper

1 large potato, peeled, and cut into ¾- to 1-inch (2- to 2.5-cm) cubes

½ cup (20g) basil leaves, thinly sliced, as garnish

• Heat the oil in a large saucepan or soup pot over medium-low heat. Add the onions, leeks, carrots, celery, and garlic and cook for 10 minutes. Stir occasionally. If the vegetables start to brown, turn down the heat.

• Meanwhile, drain one can of the beans and rinse them well. Transfer the beans to the bowl of a food processor. Add 1 cup (240ml) of water to the bowl and purée until the mixture is completely smooth. Set it aside.

• Add the tomatoes to the saucepan and turn the heat up to medium. Cook for 8 minutes, stirring often. Add the zucchini, squash, kale, and thyme and cook for 5 minutes over medium-low heat. Add the salt and pepper, remaining 6 cups water, bean purée, and potatoes. Bring to a boil, add the second can of drained beans, and then simmer the soup on low heat, covered, for 20 to 25 minutes, stirring occasionally, until the squash and potatoes are barely fork-tender.

• Adjust seasonings if needed, add fresh basil, and serve.

Cleaning Leeks

Trim the end off the white part, cut off the dark green part, and discard both. Slice the leek lengthwise and discard the two outermost layers. Slice through another layer or two, open them, and rinse off, checking for sand. If you find any, cut into the next layer and rinse it well. Continue until no sand remains.

BLACK BEAN SOUP

Parve, Gluten-free, Vegan • Serves 8 to 10

Black beans are considered one of the healthiest foods you can eat. Feel free to add any other chopped raw vegetable, corn kernels, or even whole black beans to the garnish. Since this is a puréed soup, you don't need to bother with cutting the vegetables into very small pieces.

PREP TIME: 10 minutes • COOK TIME: 40 minutes • ADVANCE PREP: May be made 3 days in advance or frozen • EQUIPMENT: Measuring cups and spoons, cutting board, knife, vegetable peeler, can opener, colander, large saucepan or soup pot, silicone spatula, food processor, ladle

SOUP

3 tablespoons sunflower, safflower, or canola oil

2 large onions, halved and sliced

4 stalks celery, roughly chopped

3 carrots, peeled and chopped into 1-inch (2.5-cm) pieces

½ jalapeño pepper, seeded and sliced

5 cloves garlic, roughly chopped

1 teaspoon dried thyme leaves

1 teaspoon garlic powder

¾ teaspoon ground cumin

½ teaspoon chili powder

½ teaspoon salt

¼ teaspoon black pepper

2 large tomatoes, seeded and chopped

½ cup (20g) cilantro leaves

1 26.5-ounce (750-g) can plus one 15.5-ounce (440-g) can black beans, drained and rinsed

5 cups (1.2L) water, or more, if soup becomes too thick

GARNISH

3 scallions, ends trimmed, thinly sliced

½ red bell pepper, finely chopped into ¼-inch (6-mm) cubes

½ yellow bell pepper, finely chopped into ¼-inch (6-mm) cubes

16 cherry tomatoes, quartered

1 avocado, cubed

Handful cilantro leaves

• Heat the oil in a large saucepan or soup pot over medium heat. Add the onions, celery, carrots, jalapeños, and garlic and cook for 10 minutes, until onions are clear. Stir occasionally. Add the thyme, garlic powder, cumin, chili powder, salt, and black pepper, and cook for another 5 minutes. Add the tomatoes and cilantro leaves, raise the heat to medium-high, and stir. Add beans and water.

• Bring the mixture to a boil, reduce the heat to low, cover, and simmer for 30 minutes, stirring occasionally. Let cool for 10 minutes. Using an immersion blender or a food processor, purée the mixture for 5 full minutes. If you're using a food processor, purée the mixture in batches.

• To serve the soup, ladle it into bowls and pass around the garnishes in separate bowls.

Canned versus Dried Beans

Canned and dried beans have the same nutritional value, though some brands add salt, so look for brands that are sodium-free. People use canned beans for convenience because they cook faster, but canned beans cost more. If you are using dried beans in a recipe that calls for canned beans, you will need to cook the beans separately until they are edible and no longer hard. After the beans have soaked overnight, drain, rinse, and then place into a saucepan and cover with water about 2 inches above the beans. Cook for 40 to 90 minutes, until soft. Skim off any dirty foam that rises to the top. You can cool and then freeze the cooked beans to use later.

MOROCCAN LENTIL SOUP

Parve, Gluten-free, Vegan • Serves 10

When I do cooking demonstrations around the world, I often try to connect food or desserts to that week's parashah, the weekly Torah portion that is read in synagogue. Some weeks are easy, such as when Abraham tells Sarah to "make haste" and prepare foods for the three angels, but other passages are impossible to connect to what I am teaching. This, however, is the soup you should make when the parashah is Toldot, which tells the story of how Esau sold his birthright to Jacob for a bowl of lentil soup.

PREP TIME: Lentils soak 6 hours to overnight; 8 minutes • COOK TIME: 55 minutes • ADVANCE PREP: May be made 3 days in advance or frozen • EQUIPMENT: Measuring cups and spoons, cutting board, knife, vegetable peeler, garlic press, large bowl, colander, large saucepan or soup pot, immersion blender

I pound (450g) dried lentils, soaked in water to cover for 6 hours or overnight, and then drained

¼ cup (60ml) extra virgin olive oil

I large onion, chopped into ¼- to ½-inch (6- to 12-mm) pieces

I large or 2 small leeks, white and light green parts only, quartered the long way and sliced (see Tip, page 25)

2 stalks celery, cut into ¼- to ½-inch (6- to 12-mm) pieces

2 carrots, peeled and cut into ¼- to ½-inch (6- to 12-mm) pieces

4 cloves garlic, crushed

I teaspoon fresh thyme leaves

I teaspoon ground cumin

I teaspoon ground turmeric

½ teaspoon salt

½ teaspoon black pepper, divided

8 cups (2L) water

• In a large bowl, cover the lentils with water and cover for 6 hours or overnight. Drain the lentils and set aside.

• In a large saucepan or soup pot, heat the oil over medium heat. Add the onions, leeks, celery, carrots, and garlic and cook until the vegetables soften, about 10 minutes, stirring often. Add the thyme, cumin, turmeric, salt, and pepper, and cook for another 3 minutes.

• Add the drained lentils and 8 cups (2L) of water to the soup pot and bring to a boil over medium-high heat. Reduce heat to low and simmer covered for 45 minutes. Let the mixture cool for 20 minutes. Using an immersion blender, purée the soup for 10 seconds, so that just about one third of the soup is thickened. Add more salt and pepper to taste, and serve.

MODERN BORSCHT: BEET AND PARSNIP PURÉE

Parve, Gluten-free, Vegan, Passover • Serves 10

When I was growing up, borscht, or Eastern European beet soup, came in a jar, and I remember that my father, Reubin Marcus, z"l (may his memory be a blessing), was the only one in the family who ate it. I also remember eating canned beets on occasion and not really liking them. Fast-forward forty-five-plus years, and beets are now one of the trendiest vegetables, valued for their vitamin C, folate, and fiber content. You can serve this thoroughly modern soup hot or cold. When I serve it hot, I add a dollop of thick, creamy coconut milk on top of each bowl (to mimic the classic sour cream garnish) and a sprig of dill; when I serve it cold, I garnish the soup with thin round slices of a half-sour pickle.

PREP TIME: 8 minutes • COOK TIME: 35 minutes • ADVANCE PREP: May be made 3 days in advance or frozen • EQUIPMENT: Measuring cups and spoons, cutting board, knife, vegetable peeler, can opener, large saucepan or soup pot, immersion blender or food processor, ladle, teaspoon

1 tablespoon avocado, sunflower, or safflower oil

2 large onions, halved and sliced

1 pound (450g) parsnips, peeled and cut into 2-inch (5-cm) chunks

3 large beets, peeled and cut into 2-inch (5-cm) chunks

6 cups (1.4L) water

1 large bunch dill, about 1½ cups (75g) loosely packed, plus some for garnish (optional)

¼ teaspoon kosher salt

¼ teaspoon white pepper

⅓ cup (80ml) canned coconut milk (the creamy, not thin kind), optional

1 half-sour pickle, halved the long way and sliced thin, for garnish (optional)

• In a large saucepan or soup pot, heat the oil over medium heat and add the onions. Cook, stirring occasionally, for 5 minutes, or until the onions look translucent. Add the parsnips, beets, and water and bring to a boil over medium-high heat. Skim off any dirty foam. Add the dill, salt, and white pepper, and reduce the heat to low; simmer covered for 30 minutes, or until the vegetables are soft.

• Purée the mixture for a full 5 minutes using an immersion blender, or purée in batches in a food processor. Add more salt and white pepper to taste.

• Serve the soup hot with a dollop of creamy coconut milk and a sprig of dill, or cold with sliced pickles, if desired.

SPLIT PEA SOUP WITH BARLEY AND PINK BEANS

Parve, Vegan • Serves 10

Split pea is one of my favorite soups to order in a kosher deli, where it usually comes very thick and is served with croutons. When I was growing up, my mother would put slices of hot dogs in the soup to mimic the chunks of ham featured in non-kosher split pea soup recipes. As a kid, I was certain that adding hot dogs to any dish was a good idea. In my updated version, to remind me of Mom's recipe, I've added pink, speckled Roman beans. This soup takes a long time to cook, because you want to make sure all the peas are cooked thoroughly before turning off the heat.

PREP TIME: Peas and beans soak 8 hours or overnight; 8 minutes • COOK TIME: 2¼ hours • ADVANCE PREP: May be made 3 days in advance or frozen • EQUIPMENT: Measuring cups and spoons, cutting board, knife, vegetable peeler, large bowl, colander, large saucepan or soup pot, silicone spatula

1 pound (450g) green split peas, soaked in 8 cups water overnight

½ cup (90g) Roman beans, soaked in the bowl with the peas

3 tablespoons extra virgin olive oil

1 large onion, chopped into ½-inch (12-mm) pieces

2 stalks celery, chopped into ½-inch (12-mm) pieces

2 large carrots, peeled and chopped into ½-inch (12-mm) pieces

1 teaspoon ground turmeric

1 teaspoon dried thyme

1 teaspoon salt, or more to taste

½ teaspoon white pepper, or more to taste

8 cups (2L) water

¼ cup (50g) pearled barley

Few sprigs fresh thyme, for garnish (optional)

• In a large bowl, place the split peas and beans and 8 cups of water. Cover and soak for 8 hours or overnight. Drain and set aside.

• In a large saucepan or soup pot, heat the oil over medium-high heat. Add the onions, celery, and carrots and cook for 5 minutes, or until they soften, stirring occasionally.

• Add the turmeric, thyme, salt, and white pepper, stir, and then cook for 1 minute. Add the split peas, beans, and water and bring to a boil. Skim off any dirty-looking foam. Add the barley, reduce the heat to low, cover, and simmer for 2 hours, or until peas are soft. Stir the soup every 15 minutes.

• Taste and add more salt and white pepper, if you like. If the soup becomes too thick on the second day, add a little water (¼ cup [60ml] at a time) to thin it out.

VIETNAMESE CHICKEN NOODLE SOUP

Meat, Gluten-Free   Serves 10

This is my kosher version of Vietnamese pho soup. I basically took my favorite chicken soup recipe and added ginger and cilantro stems during the cooking, and then added other Asian ingredients after the soup was strained. You can use your own favorite chicken soup recipe and then simply add the other ingredients to create an Asian-flavored broth. I have served this soup for a weeknight dinner. I like rice noodles, but my twins prefer wheat udon noodles.

PREP TIME: 12 minutes • COOK TIME: 2½ hours • ADVANCE PREP: May be made 3 days in advance or frozen • EQUIPMENT: Cutting board, knife, colander, vegetable peeler, measuring cups and spoons, large saucepan or soup pot, large spoon, medium saucepan, fork, slotted spoon, large sieve, small bowl, tongs, ladle

SOUP

1 whole chicken, cut into quarters or 8 pieces

2 leeks, rinsed and light green and white parts cut into quarters (see Tip, page 25)

3 stalks celery, halved

1 fennel bulb, halved

1 large onion, quartered

1 large turnip, peeled and cut into quarters

3 carrots, peeled and cut into thirds

3-inch piece of ginger, peeled and cut into 1-inch (2.5-cm) pieces (about 2 ounces [60g])

4 cloves garlic, unpeeled

12 cups water

1 tablespoon black peppercorns

1 bunch cilantro leaves and stems, divided, leaves reserved for garnish

⅓ cup (80ml) tamari soy sauce

4 teaspoons dark miso paste

¼ teaspoon ground ginger

¼ teaspoon black pepper, or more to taste

Hot chili sauce of your choice (optional)

GARNISH

1½ cups (135g) broccoli florets

1 8-ounce package (225-g) rice noodles or other noodles

6 scallions, ends trimmed, sliced

1 red Thai chili, thinly sliced

Hot chili sauce of your choice (optional)

• To make the soup, place the chicken pieces into a large saucepan or soup pot. Add the leeks, celery, fennel, onions, turnips, carrots, ginger, garlic, and water and bring to a boil over high heat. Use a large spoon to skim the dirty foam off the top of the soup. Add the black peppercorns, cover the pot, reduce the heat to low, and let the soup simmer, checking after 5 minutes and skimming off any additional foam Add the cilantro stems, cover, and simmer for 2 hours.

• Meanwhile, prepare the garnishes. Bring a medium saucepan of water to a boil, and then add the broccoli. Cook it for 2 minutes, or until it is fork-tender, and then use a slotted spoon to scoop out the broccoli and transfer it to a bowl. Bring the water to a boil again. Cook the rice noodles according to package directions and drain well.

• When the soup is done, let it cool. Strain the soup through a large sieve, reserving the carrots to slice and later return to the soup when reheating it prior to serving. Reserve the chicken pieces separately.

• Add the soy sauce to the soup. Put 4 tablespoons of the soup into a small bowl and add the miso paste and ground ginger. Stir to dissolve the miso and ginger into the soup, and then return the mixture to the pot. Add pepper to taste and stir the soup. If your family likes spice, add some hot sauce to the soup.

• To serve, shred several pieces of the reserved chicken, cut the carrots on the diagonal into 1-inch (2.5-cm) chunks, and either reheat them separately or add them to the soup. Reheat the broccoli. Reheat the soup until it is very hot. Using tongs, place some noodles into each bowl. Ladle the soup over the noodles. Add some scallions, shredded chicken, cilantro, and sliced red chili to each bowl, or make a buffet of garnishes for your family or guests to create their own combinations. Serve some hot chili sauce alongside for anyone who wants the extra kick.

Cooking for 1 to 2 People or for the Elderly

Singles have often told me that they are overwhelmed by recipes that yield way more food than they could eat alone over several days. Those of us with older parents know that appetites decrease dramatically for people over age 85. For this reason, when my recipes can be made in advance and frozen, I have included freezing instructions. Buy small plastic containers or use freezer bags and divide the dish into the portion size that suits you or the people you will be serving. Remove the containers from the freezer the night before you plan to serve the food and place in the fridge to thaw. If you are making something fresh, like a salad, prepare the full recipe of the dressing but only half the vegetables, or less. Serve what you need and dress only that portion. Save the remaining dressing for another meal.

TUSCAN FARRO SOUP

Meat • Serves 8 to 10

In the summer of 2016, I spent a week at a villa in Tuscany to celebrate my friend Elena Lefkowitz's fiftieth birthday. Elena and her husband, Jay, kashered the kitchen and hired local chefs Sylvie Tanti and Mariluisa Lovari, who brought all of the kosher ingredients from Rome, to teach us Italian cooking every afternoon. For once, I became the student. I learned how to make fresh ravioli, spaghetti, and even "pici," a kind of pasta, every strand of which must be rolled out by hand. One afternoon we learned how to make this delicious farro soup. Our chefs made it with veal sausage, but I use a veal chop instead. You can substitute beef or lamb, if you prefer.

PREP TIME: Farro soaks for 30 minutes; soup is best when it sits for 2 hours after cooking •
COOK TIME: 1½ hours • ADVANCE PREP: May be made 3 days in advance or frozen • EQUIPMENT: Measuring cups and spoons, vegetable peeler, cutting board, knife, small bowl, colander, large saucepan or soup pot

1 cup (200g) farro

2 tablespoons extra virgin olive oil

2 carrots, peeled and cut into small dice, about ⅓-inch (8-mm) pieces

2 stalks celery, cut into small dice, about ⅓-inch (8-mm) pieces

2 medium onions, cut into small dice, about ⅓-inch (8-mm) pieces

1 veal chop (bone in), about 13 ounces (370g), meat cut into ½-inch (12-mm) pieces and bone reserved

2 medium tomatoes, seeded and chopped into 1-inch (2.5-cm) pieces

6 cups (1.4L) water

3 sprigs rosemary, leaves finely chopped

16 sage leaves, chopped

1 teaspoon dried sage leaves

1 teaspoon salt

½ teaspoon black pepper

• Place the farro in a small bowl, and cover with water. Soak for 30 minutes, then drain.

• While the farro is soaking, heat the oil in a large saucepan or soup pot over medium-high heat and add the carrots, celery, and onions. Cook for 10 minutes, stirring occasionally. Add veal and the reserved bone and cook for 5 minutes. Add tomatoes and cook for 5 more minutes.

• Add the drained farro and water and bring to a boil. Reduce the heat to low and add the rosemary, fresh and dried sage, salt, and pepper. Cover and cook the soup for 1¼ hours, stirring occasionally, until it looks very creamy. Turn off the heat and let the soup sit for at least 2 hours before reheating and then serving it. Add more salt and pepper if needed. The soup may need an additional ½ cup (120ml) water the second day, if it becomes very thick.

BOUILLABAISSE

Fish, Parve • Serves 8 to 10

Bouillabaisse is a fish stew that is popular in the South of France and is typically made with shellfish. I have always wanted to develop a kosher version and created a soup, rather than a stew, that is just as filling. It has all the flavors of the original as well—fennel, orange, tomato, and anise—but I use several types of kosher fish to replace the shellfish and supply a variety of textures. Purple potatoes mimic the black mussels, and red peppers mimic the shrimp in the stew.

PREP TIME: 15 minutes • COOK TIME: 45 minutes • ADVANCE PREP: Broth may be made 3 days in advance or frozen • EQUIPMENT: Measuring cups and spoons, cutting board, knife, vegetable peeler, citrus juicer, large saucepan or soup pot, immersion blender or food processor, aluminum foil, jelly roll pan or roasting pan, ladle

SOUP

2 tablespoons extra virgin olive oil

2 leeks, white and light green parts only, sliced (see Tip, page 25)

1 large onion, halved and sliced

6 cloves garlic, roughly chopped

2 large tomatoes, seeded and chopped

1 fennel bulb, trimmed, halved, and sliced

2 bay leaves

Peel of 1 small orange, scraped off with a vegetable peeler in large pieces

1 teaspoon saffron threads

3 tablespoons pastis or Pernod (licorice-flavored liqueur), divided

3 ounces (85g) skinless flounder fillets

5 cups (1.2L) water

1 tablespoon fresh orange juice, from peeled orange

¼ teaspoon salt

⅛ teaspoon black pepper

Pinch cayenne pepper

GARNISH

2 red bell peppers, cut into 1½-inch (4-cm) pieces

4 fresh artichoke hearts cut into 2-inch (5-cm) pieces

8 small purple or red potatoes, cut into quarters

About 1 pound (450g) fish: a combination of tuna, salmon, and a white fish, cut into ½-inch (12-mm) chunks

2 tablespoons extra virgin olive oil to drizzle on top

Fennel fronds, for garnish (optional)

• To make the soup, heat the oil in a large saucepan or soup pot over medium heat and add the leeks, onions, garlic, tomatoes, and fennel, and cook for 15 minutes, stirring occasionally. Add bay leaves, orange peel, saffron, 2 tablespoons pastis, flounder, and water and bring to a boil.

• Reduce the heat to low and cook, covered, for 20 minutes, or until vegetables are soft. Remove bay leaves. Let cool for 10 minutes and then purée soup with an immersion blender for a full 3 minutes, or blend in batches in a food processor until very smooth. Add the orange juice, the remaining 1 tablespoon pastis, salt, and pepper to taste. Add cayenne. Taste to correct seasonings. May be made 2 days in advance.

• To make the garnish, preheat oven to broil. Place the bell peppers, artichokes, potato wedges, and fish on a foil-lined jelly roll pan. Drizzle with 2 tablespoons olive oil and use your hands to coat. Roast for 10 minutes, or until peppers are black on the edges and the fish is cooked.

• To serve, reheat the soup and ladle it into bowls. Place some of the pieces of the artichoke and peppers, along with the potatoes and at least one of each type of the fish chunks on top of the soup and garnish with a frond of fennel, if you like.

FRENCH ONION SOUP WITH FLANKEN

Meat, Gluten-free, Passover (without parve cheese) • Serves 8 to 10

French onion soup is one of the most perfect soups to serve on a really cold day. The classic, non-kosher French version includes toasted baguette and cheese on top. Now that parve cheeses are available, feel free to sprinkle some on top.

PREP TIME: 30 minutes; let soup cool 30 minutes before shredding meat • COOK TIME: 1¾ hours • ADVANCE PREP: May be made 3 days in advance or frozen • EQUIPMENT: Measuring cups and spoons, cutting board, knife, large saucepan or soup pot, wooden spoon, tongs

¼ cup (60ml) sunflower, safflower, or extra virgin olive oil

3 pounds (1.5kg) yellow onions, halved and sliced into ½-inch (12-mm) slices, about 10 cups

4 cloves garlic, roughly chopped

2 pounds (1kg) top rib, on the bone (flanken)

6 cups (1.4L) water

1 sprig fresh rosemary

2 sprigs fresh thyme

½ teaspoon salt

1 teaspoon black pepper

• Using your widest soup pot (the larger the pot, the better it is for browning), heat the oil over medium-high heat. Add the onions and cook them for 30 minutes, stirring every 4 to 5 minutes, until they are well browned but not burned. Reduce the heat if they start to burn. Add the garlic and cook for another 5 minutes.

• Move the onions to the side of the pot and add the meat, trying to fit all the meat on the bottom of the pot. If you reduced the heat while cooking the onions, raise it back to medium-high. Using tongs, brown the meat on both sides, for 3 minutes total.

• Add the water, rosemary, and thyme, and bring the mixture to a boil. Reduce the heat to low, add the salt and pepper, cover the pot, and cook for 1¼ hours, or until the meat is soft. Let the soup cool for 30 minutes. Remove the stems from the rosemary and thyme.

• Remove the meat from the soup and use your hands or a knife to shred the meat, discarding any visible fat. Place the meat back into the soup pot. Taste and add more salt and pepper if desired and reheat to serve.

TZATZIKI SOUP

Dairy, Vegetarian, Passover • Serves 6 to 8

This soup has the flavor of the classic Greek side dish. Serve it on a really hot day, as it is very refreshing and also packs a lot of nutrition.

PREP TIME: 8 minutes; 3 hours to chill • ADVANCE PREP: May be made 2 days in advance; needs 3 hours to chill • EQUIPMENT: Cutting board, knife, measuring cups and spoons, citrus juicer, food processor or blender, large bowl, ladle

2 English cucumbers, unpeeled, halved, and cut into thirds, plus 1 small cucumber or ⅓ additional English cucumber, for garnish

1 large shallot, peeled and quartered

2 cloves garlic

⅓ cup (17g) fresh dill

⅓ cup (17g) Italian parsley leaves

12 mint leaves

2 scallions, ends trimmed, divided

2 cups (480g) Greek yogurt

1 cup (240ml) water

1 tablespoon honey

1 tablespoon fresh lemon juice (from 1 lemon)

¼ teaspoon salt

Pinch white pepper

¼ cup (30g) walnut halves, crushed, for garnish (optional)

• In a food processor or blender, place two of the cucumbers, the shallots, garlic, dill, parsley, mint, one scallion, and the yogurt, water, honey, and lemon juice and purée until the soup is completely smooth. Add the salt and white pepper and process again. Taste to correct seasonings. Place the soup in a large bowl in the fridge for at least 3 hours. This may be done 2 days in advance.

• When ready to serve, cut the additional cucumber into ½-inch (12-mm) cubes and slice the remaining scallion into thin slices. Ladle the soup into bowls and garnish with some cucumbers and scallions. Sprinkle the crushed walnuts on top, if desired.

WATERMELON, PEACH, AND MINT GAZPACHO

Parve, Gluten-free, Passover • Serves 10

This refreshing summer soup is best served with a watermelon, scallion, and avocado garnish, so don't skimp on that. For adult guests, I sometimes add a few teaspoons of ice-cold vodka or tequila to the soup.

PREP TIME: 8 minutes; 4 hours to chill • ADVANCE PREP: May be made 2 days in advance • EQUIPMENT: Measuring cups and spoons, cutting board, knife, citrus juicer, small bowl, food processor or blender, large bowl

8 cups (1.3kg) watermelon, cubed and divided

2 large ripe yellow peaches, unpeeled, pitted, and cut into 1½-inch (4-cm) cubes, about 4 cups

1 English cucumber, unpeeled, and cut into chunks

⅓ cup (20g) fresh mint leaves

⅓ cup (35g) chopped red onions

1 tablespoon chopped fresh ginger

Juice of ½ lime

1 tablespoon honey

½ teaspoon black pepper

3 scallions, ends trimmed, sliced, for garnish (optional)

1 ripe avocado, cubed, for garnish (optional)

• Separate 1 heaping cup of cubed watermelon from the 8 cups (1.3kg) total and chop it into ¼-inch (6-mm) cubes. Set them aside in a small bowl and chill until ready to serve.

• In batches, place the peaches, cucumbers, remaining 7 cups (1kg) watermelon, mint leaves, red onions, and ginger into a blender or food processor and purée until smooth. Transfer the mixture to a large bowl or container. Add the lime juice, honey, and pepper and stir. Chill the gazpacho for 4 hours or overnight. Garnish with the reserved cup of watermelon cubes, scallions, and avocados. You could also add sliced peaches, small-cubed cucumbers, and diced red onion in whatever combination you prefer.

Meat
Main Dishes

ARROZ CON POLLO WITH BROWN RICE AND SALSA VERDE

Meat, Gluten-free • Serves 6

If you have *The New Passover Menu*, my third cookbook, you might already know and love Betty Supo's recipe for spicy Peruvian salsa verde, her delicious green sauce. Although it was paired there with a simple Peruvian roasted chicken, here it is served the way it is meant to be—with arroz con pollo, chicken with rice. It is an entire meal in a dish. This recipe requires a little more work than most chicken recipes, but it is really worth the effort. I would suggest serving it on Sukkot.

PREP TIME: 25 minutes • COOK TIME: 55 minutes for rice; 28 minutes for chicken • ADVANCE PREP: The salsa may be made up to 1 week in advance and stored in the fridge; chicken and rice may be made 2 days in advance • EQUIPMENT: Measuring cups and spoons, cutting board, knife, small or medium saucepan, medium frying pan, silicone spatula, fork, food processor, 2 small bowls, large frying pan, tongs, Dutch oven or large saucepan

PERUVIAN GREEN RICE

2 cups (380g) brown rice

6 cups (1.4L) water, divided

4 teaspoons sunflower, safflower, or canola oil

1 large or 2 small onions, finely chopped

4 cloves garlic, roughly chopped

½ teaspoon ground turmeric

½ teaspoon ground cumin

¼ teaspoon black pepper

½ teaspoon salt, divided

1 large bunch cilantro leaves

½ jalapeño pepper, seeded

1 cup (135g) frozen peas and carrots

SALSA VERDE

2 tablespoons sunflower or safflower oil

4 cloves garlic, halved

1 medium onion, halved and sliced

2 jalapeño peppers, halved (see Tip on page 46)

1 large or 2 small bunches cilantro leaves

½ cup (120ml) water

½ teaspoon kosher salt

CHICKEN

2 teaspoons sunflower, safflower, or canola oil, divided

1 teaspoon ground turmeric

1 teaspoon ground cumin

1 teaspoon garlic powder

½ teaspoon black pepper

½ teaspoon salt

1 whole chicken, cut into 8 pieces

• In a small or medium saucepan, bring the brown rice to a boil in 4½ cups (1L) water. Cover the saucepan and simmer for 45 minutes, or until all the water has been absorbed. May be made 2 days in advance.

• While the rice is cooking, prepare the salsa verde. Heat the oil in a medium frying pan over medium-high heat. Add the garlic and cook for 1 minute. Add the onions and cook for 3 to 5 minutes over medium-high heat, or until the onions soften and are lightly browned. Add the jalapeño halves, cut side down, and cook for 1 minute. Turn them over and then cook for another 4 minutes, over medium-low heat, stirring occasionally, until the jalapeños are fork-tender.

• Let the aromatics cool for 15 minutes. Then transfer them to a food processor. Add the cilantro, water, and salt and process until the mixture is thoroughly puréed and smooth. Pour into a small bowl and set aside. May be made 1 week in advance.

• Next, to prepare the chicken, in a large frying pan heat the oil over medium-high heat. In a small bowl, combine the turmeric, cumin, garlic powder, black pepper, and salt and rub the mixture all over the chicken pieces. Place the chicken pieces into the hot pan, skin side up, and let them cook undisturbed for 4 minutes. Then turn over the pieces and brown for another 4 minutes. Remove them from the pan.

• Now return to the rice ingredients. In a large Dutch oven or large saucepan, heat 2 teaspoons of the oil over medium heat. Add the onions and cook them for 6 minutes, or until lightly browned. Add the garlic and cook for another 2 minutes. Add the turmeric, cumin, black pepper, and ¼ teaspoon salt and mix well. Place the chicken pieces on top with ½ cup (120ml) water, then cover and cook over medium heat for 20 minutes. The mixture should be bubbling the whole time.

• Transfer the chicken to a platter and cover it to keep it warm. Place the cilantro leaves, jalapeño, ¼ teaspoon salt, and ½ cup (120ml) water in the bowl of a food processor and purée for 1 minute, or until the mixture is entirely liquefied. Scrape down the sides if needed. Pour this mixture into the Dutch oven or saucepan, over the onions. Add remaining ½ cup (120ml) water to the food processor bowl, swirl it around, and then pour it into the Dutch oven or saucepan, and stir. Cook the mixture over medium-low heat for 3 minutes.

• Fluff the cooked rice, add it to the onions and green purée mixture, and then stir until it is all mixed in. Add the peas and carrots on top, cover the pot, and cook for 10 minutes over low heat. Place the chicken pieces on top of the rice and heat over low heat for another 5 to 10 minutes, or until the chicken is hot.

• To serve, scoop up some rice and chicken and plate it with the green sauce alongside.

Jalapeños

If you have fewer jalapeños than is called for in a recipe, you can use what you have and include the seeds in the dish. But add chili seeds to a recipe only if you are looking to add extra heat and intense spice.

INDIAN BARBECUED CHICKEN

Meat, Gluten-free, Passover • Serves 6

Once a year I prepare a full Indian dinner for Shabbat. About two years ago, my friend Rick Silber decided to join me. We compiled a fabulous menu that included this chicken, inspired by recipes from a community cookbook produced in Chicago by women from the Kerala region of India. It is definitely spicy, but not too spicy for me, and sadly, I cannot tolerate much spice.

PREP TIME: 5 minutes • COOK TIME: 40 to 60 minutes • ADVANCE PREP: May be made 2 days in advance • EQUIPMENT: Cutting board, knife, measuring cups and spoons, large roasting pan, food processor, silicone spatula, tongs, fork

1 chicken, cut into 8 pieces

3 scallions, ends trimmed, cut into thirds

1 medium onion, cut into quarters

2-inch (5-cm) piece fresh ginger, roughly chopped, about 2½ tablespoons chopped

½ cup (20g) packed cilantro leaves

¼ cup (60ml) fresh lemon juice (from 1 to 2 lemons)

3 tablespoons coconut oil

5 cloves garlic, chopped

1 tablespoon ground turmeric

1 teaspoon ground cardamom

¼ teaspoon salt

¼ teaspoon ground red pepper

2 jalapeños or other green chilies, seeds removed, cut into quarters

• Place the chicken in a large roasting pan that you can use later to bake the chicken. Place the scallions, onions, ginger, cilantro, lemon juice, coconut oil, garlic, turmeric, cardamom, salt, red pepper, and jalapeños into the bowl of a food processor, and process into a paste.

• Using a silicone spatula or gloved hand, spread the paste all around the chicken pieces. Cover and place the chicken in the fridge for at least 2 hours or overnight.

• If you're cooking the chicken in the oven, preheat it to broil. Turn on your outdoor grill, and when the temperature is approximately 550°F (290°C), using tongs, place the chicken pieces on the grill skin side down. Grill for about 8 to 10 minutes, and then baste the chicken with some paste, turn the chicken over, and baste it again. Grill the chicken for another 5 to 8 minutes, until both sides are well browned, but not black. Place the pieces into another pan and bake them, uncovered, for 20 minutes or until the juices run clear when the chicken is pierced with a fork.

• If you're using the oven, broil the chicken for 20 minutes, or until it is black and crispy, and then reduce the heat to 350°F (180°C). Bake the chicken for another 30 to 40 minutes or until the juices run clear when the chicken is pierced with a fork.

Unsticking Grilled Chicken

When cooking chicken pieces on the grill skin side down, after you place the pieces on the grill, count to 10 and then lift up the pieces and put them back down on the grill—this will prevent sticking. This method also works for skinless, boneless chicken.

WHOLE ROASTED CHICKEN WITH QUINOA AND PINE NUT STUFFING

Meat, Gluten-free, Passover • Serves 6

Many people find quinoa too dry. This recipe, in which about a third of the quinoa is stuffed into a whole chicken, results in a very moist side dish.

PREP TIME: 30 minutes • COOK TIME: 1 hour • ADVANCE PREP: Stuffing may be made 2 days in advance • EQUIPMENT: Measuring cups and spoons, cutting board, knife, small saucepan with lid, large frying pan with 2-inch (5-cm) sides or shallow wide saucepan, 2 small bowls, medium bowl, large roasting pan, small baking dish, aluminum foil, kitchen glove or quart-size plastic bag, tongs, fork, large spoon, kitchen scissors

STUFFING

1 cup (180g) quinoa

2 cups (480ml) water

¾ cup (100g) pine nuts

2 tablespoons extra virgin olive oil

2 stalks celery, cut into ¼-inch (6-mm) pieces

2 large shallots, chopped

3 cloves garlic, chopped

1 red bell pepper, chopped into ¼-inch (6-mm) dice

1 yellow or orange bell pepper, chopped into ¼-inch (6-mm) dice

½ teaspoon ground turmeric

½ teaspoon ground cumin

¾ teaspoon salt

½ teaspoon black pepper

CHICKEN

1 whole chicken

1 tablespoon extra virgin olive oil

½ teaspoon ground turmeric

½ teaspoon ground cumin

½ teaspoon dried thyme

¼ teaspoon ground ginger

¼ teaspoon salt

¼ teaspoon black pepper

• To make the stuffing, place the quinoa and water in a small saucepan and bring it to a boil over high heat. Reduce the heat to low, cover the pot, and simmer for 15 minutes, or until all the water has been absorbed.

• Heat a large frying pan or a shallow wide saucepan over medium heat. Add the pine nuts and cook them, stirring often, until they're toasted. Do not leave them unattended. Transfer the pine nuts to a small bowl to cool.

• In the same pan, heat the oil over medium-high heat. Add the celery, shallots, and garlic and cook for 5 minutes. Add the bell peppers, turmeric, cumin, salt, and black pepper, mix well, and cook for 5 more minutes. Add the cooked quinoa to the pan and mix it well. Cook for 5 minutes, stirring often. Transfer the mixture to a medium bowl and let it cool. May be made 2 days in advance.

• When you're ready to stuff the chicken, add the toasted pine nuts to the quinoa mixture and mix them in.

• To make the chicken, preheat the oven to 450°F (230°C). Place the chicken in a large roasting pan. Stuff as much of the quinoa mixture as you can fit into the cavity of the chicken. Place any leftover stuffing in a small baking dish, cover it with aluminum foil, and set aside. Drizzle the oil over the chicken. In a small bowl, combine the turmeric, cumin, thyme, ginger, salt, and pepper. Using a kitchen glove or a quart-size plastic bag to cover your hand, rub the mixture all over the chicken. Place the chicken, breast side down, in the roasting pan.

• Roast the chicken for 20 minutes. Using tongs, carefully turn the chicken over and roast it, breast side up, for another 20 minutes. Reduce the heat to 350°F (180°C). Add the covered pan of extra stuffing to the oven. Roast the chicken for another 20 minutes, or longer, until the juices run clear when you pierce the chicken with a fork.

• Let the chicken sit for 5 minutes. Scoop out the stuffing and combine it with the stuffing that was cooked separately. Add a little of the pan juice to the stuffing and mix it in. If you made the quinoa earlier in the day, reheat it before serving. Use kitchen scissors to cut up the chicken. Serve the chicken pieces over the stuffing and drizzle some of the pan juices over the top.

Cooking for a Large Crowd: Can Every Recipe Be Doubled without Trouble?

I often double dessert recipes without any problem. When it comes to a meat or chicken recipe where the protein in cooked in a sauce, I can double the meat or chicken amount without doubling the sauce ingredients.

COQ AU VIN BLANC

Coq au vin, French for chicken with wine, is traditionally made with red wine and is a classic winter dish. This lighter version, made with white wine, can be enjoyed year round. If you can find kumquats, use them, as they give the dish a sharp orange flavor. If kumquats are out of season, use sliced oranges cut into small triangles (keep the peel on). I have also prepared this dish with varying qualities of white wine, always with good results.

PREP TIME: 20 minutes • COOK TIME: ½ hour • ADVANCE PREP: May be made 2 days in advance • EQUIPMENT: Measuring cups and spoons, cutting board, knife, large frying pan, tongs, 9 x 13-inch (23 x 33-cm) roasting pan, large spoon, aluminum foil, small saucepan

1 tablespoon plus 2 teaspoons extra virgin olive oil, divided

1 chicken, cut into 8 pieces

3 large shallots, halved and sliced thinly

2 leeks, white and light green parts only, sliced into ¼-inch (6-mm) slices (see Tip, page 25)

1 onion, cut into ¼-inch (6-mm) slices

¼ teaspoon salt

¼ teaspoon black pepper

1 head garlic, cloves separated but unpeeled

1 bottle (750 ml) white wine

3 sprigs fresh rosemary

6 sprigs fresh thyme

1 tablespoon chopped fresh tarragon

10 kumquats, each sliced into 4 pieces, or 3⅓-inch (8-mm) orange slices, peel intact, cut into 8 triangles

8 to 10 ounces (225 to 280g) pearl onions

• Preheat the oven to 350°F (180°C). In a large frying pan, heat 2 teaspoons of the olive oil over medium-high heat. Using tongs, add the chicken in batches and brown it well on both sides, about 4 minutes per side. Place the browned chicken into a 9 x 13-inch (23 x 33-cm) roasting pan.

• Reduce the heat to medium-low and add the remaining 1 tablespoon of the oil to the frying pan.

Place the shallots, leeks, and onions in the pan and cook them, scraping up the browned bits from the chicken, for about 6 to 8 minutes, until they start to brown. Add salt and pepper and stir.

• Scoop the shallot, leek, and onion mixture out of the frying pan and place it under the chicken pieces in the roasting pan. Do not wash the frying pan. Scatter the garlic cloves around the chicken. Pour the wine on top. Add the rosemary and thyme sprigs and sprinkle the tarragon over the chicken pieces. Place the kumquats or orange pieces on top of the chicken.

• Cover the roasting pan tightly with aluminum foil and bake for 1 hour.

• Meanwhile, bring a small saucepan of water to a boil, add the pearl onions, boil them for 2 minutes, then drain off the water. When the onions are cool enough to handle, cut off their ends and squeeze them out of their skins. Heat the unwashed frying pan over medium heat and add the pearl onions. Cook them for about 5 minutes, shaking the pan often, so that the onions brown on all sides. Set the pan aside.

• After the chicken has cooked for 1 hour, remove the foil, add the pearl onions and cook for another 30 minutes, uncovered, and serve.

SAGE AND SHALLOT ROAST TURKEY WITH WHOLE-WHEAT STUFFING

Meat, Passover (just turkey, not stuffing) • Turkey breast serves 6; stuffing serves 10

Thanksgiving Day was the second to last day of shiva for my mother in 2015. It also happened to be my parents' wedding anniversary. We didn't know what was appropriate to do: We needed dinner, and my children wanted Thanksgiving food, yet we didn't want to feel like we were celebrating. My mother-in-law and sister-in-law ordered roast turkey and simple sides, although a full kosher Thanksgiving meal showed up. All day long I was dreading how sad it would be to be together for a holiday without Mom. As it turned out, two of my closest friends and their families came by to pay a shiva call right when we were sitting down to eat. The house became hectic as we added more chairs to the table and set up tables for the teens in other rooms of the house. Rather than eating a somber meal, we felt enveloped by love and comfort, precisely the goal of shiva and what my mother would have wanted for us.

Note: *If you are making a whole turkey, double the rub ingredients.*

PREP TIME: 20 minutes • COOK TIME: 1 hour 20 minutes for turkey breast, 15 minutes per pound for whole turkey • ADVANCE PREP: Stuffing may be made 1 day in advance • EQUIPMENT: Measuring cups and spoons, cutting board, knife, large frying pan or wide saucepan, large roasting pan, 9 x 13-inch (23 x 33-cm) baking pan, small bowl, aluminum foil, meat forks, carving knife, sieve, silicone spatula

STUFFING

¼ cup (60ml) extra virgin olive oil

1 large onion, chopped into ½-inch (12-mm) pieces

1 shallot, finely chopped

4 stalks celery (include leaves), chopped into ½-inch (12-mm) pieces

1 large green apple, peeled and chopped into ½-inch (12-mm) pieces

2 teaspoons dried thyme leaves

2 teaspoons dried sage leaves

8 cups (3kg) whole-wheat bread cubes, or stale Whole-Wheat Onion Challah (see page 133)

¾ cup (100g) dried cranberries

½ cup (120ml) Port, Marsala, or red wine

½ cup (120ml) water or homemade chicken stock

¼ teaspoon salt

¼ teaspoon black pepper

TURKEY

1 5- to 6-pound (2.3- to 2.7-kg) turkey breast

1 large shallot, halved and finely chopped

½ cup (18g) loosely packed fresh sage leaves

2 tablespoons extra virgin olive oil

⅛ teaspoon salt

¼ teaspoon black pepper

• Preheat oven to 450°F (230°C).

• To prepare the stuffing, heat the oil over medium-high heat in a large frying pan or wide saucepan. Add the onions, shallots, and celery and cook for 10 to 12 minutes, or until vegetables are soft.

• Meanwhile, rinse and dry the turkey and place it in a large roasting pan. In a small bowl, mix the shallot, sage, olive oil, salt, and pepper and mix well. Rub the mixture all over the turkey, inside and out. Add more pepper if desired. Roast the turkey for 20 minutes. (If you're using a whole turkey, prepare the stuffing first and let it cool before stuffing the turkey.)

• When the vegetables for the stuffing are soft, add the apple, thyme, and sage and cook the mixture for another 3 minutes. Add the bread cubes and cranberries and toss well. Cook for 2 minutes and keep mixing. Add the wine, water or stock, salt, and pepper, and stir and cook the mixture for another 2 minutes. It can be made 1 day in advance and stored in the fridge.

• After the turkey has browned, turn the oven down to 325°F (160°C) and roast the turkey for another hour, or until the juices run clear and a thermometer reads 160°F (70°C). Place the stuffing into a 9 x 13-inch (23 x 33-cm) baking pan, cover it with aluminum foil, and bake it at the same time as the turkey, on another rack in the oven, or separately, later on, for 45 minutes to 1 hour. If you're roasting a whole turkey, roast it for 15 minutes per pound, or until the juices run clear. You can also test doneness by jiggling one of the turkey legs: If it comes away easily from the side of the bird, it's done.

• Using meat forks, transfer the turkey to a platter or cutting board and let it rest 15 to 20 minutes before carving. To make the gravy, add ½ cup (120ml) hot water to the roasting pan, stir it into the pan juices using a silicone spatula, and then strain it through a sieve into a bowl or gravy boat. Reheat if necessary.

• Serve the turkey hot with stuffing and gravy, or cold in salads and sandwiches.

Thawing Frozen Meat and Turkey

The safest way to defrost meat is to plan ahead and thaw it in the fridge overnight. To thaw faster, soak the wrapped meat in cold water for a few hours. Some people soak wrapped meat in hot water, but only do that for less than 9 minutes. You can also use the "defrost" setting on the microwave, but be careful not to let the meat cook. A whole turkey should thaw for two days in the fridge.

BAKED SCHNITZEL WITH NUT CRUST

Meat, Gluten-free, Passover • Serves 4 to 6 (8–10 slices)

My goal with this recipe was to bake it first, rather than frying it, and then see if I could come up with a gluten-free coating that everyone would love. This schnitzel is great cold after the first day. It should be made after Passover when, if you're anything like me, you'll have leftover ground nuts in your pantry. You can also use the same baking method with your favorite schnitzel breadcrumbs.

PREP TIME: 10 minutes • COOK TIME: 15 minutes • ADVANCE PREP: May be made 3 days in advance or frozen • EQUIPMENT: Measuring cups and spoons, cutting board, knife, 2 jelly roll pans, food processor, 2 shallow bowls, gallon-size freezer bag or shallow bowl, large plate, tongs

2 to 2½ pounds (910g to 1.2kg) chicken scaloppini (thin slices), about 10 pieces

3 tablespoons sunflower oil, divided

1 cup (120g) shelled pistachios

1 cup (120g) slivered almonds

½ cup (45g) ground hazelnuts (filberts)

1½ teaspoons ground turmeric

2 teaspoons ground cumin

2 teaspoons paprika

2½ teaspoons ground ginger

2 teaspoons garlic powder

¼ teaspoon cayenne pepper

½ teaspoon kosher salt

¼ teaspoon black pepper

2–3 large eggs, as needed to coat all the pieces

1 cup (110g) chickpea flour (or potato starch)

Sprigs of Italian parsley, for garnish (optional)

• Preheat the oven to 475–480°F (245–250°C). Place 1½ tablespoons of oil on each of 2 jelly roll pans and spread to coat. Place the pistachios, almonds, and ground hazelnuts into the bowl of a food processor. Add the turmeric, cumin, paprika, ginger, garlic powder, cayenne, salt, and black pepper. Process until the nuts have been reduced to very small pieces, but not ground into a powder. Place them in a shallow bowl.

• Crack two of the eggs into a shallow bowl and beat them well. Place the chickpea flour into a gallon-size freezer bag or a shallow bowl (the freezer bag works well). Cut the chicken into as many pieces as you like and, using your fingers, dip each into the chickpea flour to coat it completely, shaking off any excess. Then dip the pieces into the beaten eggs and press them into the nut mixture to completely coat the chicken. Place the chicken on a large plate and set it aside. Wash your hands with warm soapy water.

• When the oven is preheated, place the oil-coated pans into the oven and heat for 5 minutes. When the jelly roll pans are hot, very carefully remove one pan at a time and add the chicken, leaving a little room between each piece so that they don't touch each other. Put the pans back in the oven and bake the chicken for 10 minutes. Using tongs, turn over the pieces and bake them for another 5 minutes. Rotate the pans halfway through the cooking time so that each pan has a turn on the bottom rack to ensure maximum crunchiness. Serve immediately.

BRISKET BOURGUIGNON

Meat, Gluten-free, Passover • Serves 10 to 12

This recipe is inspired by Julia Child's famous beef bourguignon recipe, which is featured in the film *Julie and Julia*. In that movie, Julia's story is also my story: I was living in Europe with a diplomat husband and thought, "Why not? I'll go to cooking school." Then I started teaching cooking classes in my small European apartment, as Julia did. I came to book writing later, and, like Julia, it took some time to get that first book published. Even now, when I recall the scene in the film when she pulls the published book out of its packaging, I just want to cry for joy.

PREP TIME: 10 minutes • COOK TIME: 3 hours • ADVANCE PREP: May be made 3 days in advance or frozen • EQUIPMENT: Paper towels, measuring cups and spoons, cutting board(s), knife, vegetable peeler, garlic press, large Dutch oven, tongs, plate, large roasting pan, aluminum foil, colander, carving knife, small saucepan, medium frying pan or saucepan, medium bowl, silicone spatula, fork

BRISKET

3 tablespoons extra virgin olive oil, divided

3 tablespoons potato starch

5 pounds second-cut brisket, rinsed and dried very well with paper towels

3 carrots, peeled and sliced

2 onions, halved and cut into ½-inch (12-mm) slices

2 medium tomatoes, seeds removed and chopped into 1-inch (2.5-cm) pieces

3 cloves garlic, crushed

1 teaspoon fresh thyme leaves

2 bay leaves

1 bottle (750 ml) dry red wine

½ teaspoon salt

½ teaspoon black pepper

ONIONS AND MUSHROOMS

8 to 10 ounces (225 to 280g) pearl onions

8 to 10 ounces (225 to 280g) button mushrooms

2 tablespoons extra virgin olive oil, divided

1 tablespoon finely chopped Italian flat parsley

Pinch salt

• Preheat the oven to 375°F (190°C). Heat 1 tablespoon of the olive oil in a large Dutch oven over medium-high heat. Sprinkle potato starch on both sides of the meat, shaking off any excess, and brown the meat in the pan on both sides until you see crispy parts on the meat, after about 8 minutes. Using a fork, transfer the meat to a plate.

• Reduce the heat to medium. Add the remaining 2 tablespoons of oil, carrots, and onions to the Dutch oven and cook them for 8 minutes over medium heat, stirring often. Add the tomatoes, garlic, thyme, and bay leaves and cook for 2 minutes. Place the meat in a large roasting pan. Add the wine and bring the mixture to a boil. Add the salt and pepper. Cover the pan tightly with aluminum foil and bake the meat in the oven for 1½ hours.

• While the meat is cooking, prepare the pearl onions and mushrooms. Bring a small saucepan of water to a boil. Add the onions and cook them for 2 minutes. Drain off the water, and when the onions are cool enough the handle, snip off the ends and press the onions out of their skins.

56 • THE HEALTHY JEWISH KITCHEN

• Heat 1 tablespoon of the oil in a medium frying or saucepan over medium heat. Cook the onions until they're browned on all sides, 4 to 5 minutes. Transfer the onions to a medium bowl. Add another tablespoon of oil to the pan and cook the mushrooms over medium-high heat for about 5 minutes, or until browned, stirring often. Add a pinch of salt. Add the mushrooms to the bowl with the onions.

• Remove the roasting pan from the oven and place the meat on a cutting board. Using a carving knife, slice it against the grain to make thin slices. Reduce the heat to 350°F (180°C). Return the slices to the pan and immerse them in the liquid. Cover and bake the meat for another hour. Add the mushrooms and onions to the sauce. Cover the pan and return it to the oven. Bake the meat, covered, for another half hour or longer, until it is soft when pierced with a fork. Taste the sauce and add salt and pepper, if needed. Sprinkle the meat with parsley and serve.

Searing Meat

Searing intensifies the flavor of meat. The moisture on the surface of the meat evaporates, and the creation of a caramelized crust results in more flavor compounds. After you place the meat into the hot pan, wait until the meat releases from the pan on its own, and then turn it over to sear the other side.

FEIJOADA: BRAZILIAN CHOLENT WITH COLLARD GREENS AND FAROFA

Meat, Gluten-free • Serves 10 to 12

Feijoada is the national dish of Brazil, typically made with pork and several of the most inexpensive parts of the pig. I was determined to make it kosher. After cooking it on the stovetop, I wondered how it would taste if I slow-cooked it for many hours like cholent. I discovered that it is even better that way. You can use a slow cooker to make this version of feijoada (just be sure to reduce the amount of water by 1 cup [240ml]). You can also use any cuts of red meat or veal your butcher may have on hand; the idea is to combine different textures. In Brazil, they also add sliced sausage to the dish. The amount of meat you use is also approximate—adding or decreasing by a few ounces of meat will still result in a great dish. Typically, collard greens and farofa are served alongside the feijoada. But if you cannot find manioc flour (made from yucca or cassava) to make the farofa, you can certainly enjoy the dish without it. Brazilians also serve orange wedges and white rice with feijoada.

PREP TIME: 8 minutes • COOK TIME: 8 hours to overnight • ADVANCE PREP: Stew may be made 3 days in advance or frozen; collard greens may be made 1 day in advance; farofa may be made 2 days in advance • EQUIPMENT: Measuring cups and spoons, cutting board, knife, large Dutch oven with ovenproof lid, silicone spatula, wooden spoon, large frying pan or wide saucepan, tongs, 2 medium bowls

STEW

1 tablespoon sunflower, safflower, canola, or olive oil

1 large onion, chopped into ½-inch (12-mm) pieces

3 stalks celery, chopped into ½-inch (12-mm) pieces

3 cloves garlic, roughly chopped

1 pound (450g) black beans (you can soak them overnight if you'd like to reduce gassiness, but that step is not necessary for this dish)

1 pound (450g) beef shank

10 ounces (280g) beef cubes

1 pound (450g) veal shank or cubes

8 ounces (225g) top rib (flanken) on the bone, cut into 3-inch (7.5-cm) pieces

3 bay leaves, fresh or dried

5 cups (1.2L) water

COLLARD GREENS

1 tablespoon extra virgin olive oil

2 cloves garlic, roughly chopped

1½ pounds (680g) collard greens, stacked and sliced into ½-inch (12-mm) ribbons, divided

Salt and black pepper to taste

FAROFA

4 tablespoons extra virgin olive oil

1 small onion, finely chopped

1 cup (120g) manioc flour

Salt and black pepper

• Preheat the oven to 225°F (105°C).

• To make the stew, in a large Dutch oven, heat the oil over medium-high heat. Add the onions and celery and cook for 5 minutes, until they start to brown. Add the garlic and cook for another 2 minutes. Add the beans, all the meat, bay leaves, and water and bring to a boil. With a wooden spoon, skim off any grayish foam from the top of the stew.

• Cover and place in the oven for 8 to 10 hours or overnight. Every once in a while, open the cover and press the beans down into the liquid.

• To make the collard greens, heat the oil in a large frying pan or wide saucepan over medium heat, and add the garlic. When the garlic starts to brown, add half of the greens and cook them, using tongs to stir and turn the greens until they start to cook down. Add the other half of the greens and toss them, moving the uncooked greens to the bottom of the pan. Cook the greens for about 5 minutes, until all of the leaves are shiny. Add salt and pepper to taste and stir. Place in a medium bowl and set aside.

• To make the farofa, heat the oil in a large frying pan or wide saucepan over medium-high heat. Add the onions and cook for about 5 minutes, just until they start to brown. Add the manioc flour and cook it, stirring often, for 5 to 7 minutes or until the flour is toasted. Add salt and pepper to taste. Place in a medium bowl. May be made 2 days in advance.

• Serve the feijoada right from the pot with the collard greens and farofa, and some cooked rice in a separate bowl. Finish each plate with a couple orange wedges.

GRILLED STEAK WITH EVERYTHING MARINADE

Meat, Gluten-free, Passover (omit soy sauce and mustard) • Serves 4 to 6

This is one of those non-recipe recipes. Every time I grill a large piece of meat and want a marinade, I just open my spice cabinet and go a little crazy, adding a little of this and a little bit of that. So you can imagine how it pained me to stop and measure everything to create this recipe. Feel free to add spices you like and omit any from my list that you dislike or simply don't have in your pantry. I typically use different spices every time I grill a steak, and haven't made a bad one yet.

PREP TIME: 5 minutes; marinate for 6 hours or overnight, if possible • COOK TIME: 16 to 20 minutes •
ADVANCE PREP: Meat may be marinated or cooked 2 days in advance • EQUIPMENT: Measuring cups and spoons, whisk, large container or gallon plastic bag, tongs, 9 x 13-inch (23 x 33-cm) roasting pan

3 pounds (1.4kg) London broil or flank steak

¼ cup (60ml) extra virgin olive oil

1 tablespoon apple cider vinegar

1 tablespoon honey

2 tablespoons tamari soy sauce

¼ cup (60ml) water

¼ cup (60ml) orange juice

1 tablespoon garlic powder

1 tablespoon paprika

1 tablespoon ground cumin

2 teaspoons onion powder

2 teaspoons ground mustard

2 teaspoons dried oregano

2 teaspoons dried basil

2 bay leaves

2 teaspoons dried thyme leaves

1 teaspoon ground turmeric

½ teaspoon black pepper

¼ teaspoon chili powder

• Measure the olive oil in a 2-cup (500ml) liquid measuring cup. Add the vinegar, honey, soy sauce, water, and orange juice to the cup and whisk it well. Pour the mixture into a large container or gallon plastic bag. Add the garlic powder, paprika, cumin, onion powder, ground mustard, oregano, basil, bay leaves, thyme, turmeric, pepper, and chili powder and mix.

• Add the meat to the container or plastic bag and make sure all sides are coated with the marinade. Cover the container or seal the bag and let the meat marinate in the fridge for 6 hours or overnight.

• Preheat the grill to 550°F (290°C). Lift the meat out of the marinade and place it on the grill. Cook for 10 minutes. Pour a little marinade on the meat. Turn the meat over, pour some more marinade on the cooked side, and cook the meat for another 6 to 10 minutes for medium doneness.

• Pour the remaining marinade into a 9 x 13-inch (23 x 33-cm) roasting pan and bring to a boil, then reduce to a simmer. Place into a roasting pan. When the meat is cooked, put it back in the cooked marinade and turn it over to coat it evenly.

• Slice the meat against the grain, making thin slices, and serve.

JAPANESE LAMB CHOPS

Meat • Serves 3 to 4, makes 8 to 12 lamb chops

During the summer of 2015 I ate a delicious meal at the Lumina restaurant at the Carlton Hotel in Tel Aviv. My brother Ezra Marcus ordered Japanese veal ribs, which were moist and flavorful, and they gave me the idea for this recipe. When grilling lamb chops, make sure the heat does not get too high, or the dripping fat can cause large flames on the grill and then your pricey kosher lamb chops will get completely charred.

PREP TIME: 5 minutes; let marinate 4 hours or overnight, if possible • COOK TIME: 7 to 9 minutes
• ADVANCE PREP: Chops may be marinated or cooked 2 days in advance, but best fresh •
EQUIPMENT: Microplane zester, citrus juicer, measuring cups and spoons, cutting board, knife, food processor, large container or gallon resealable plastic bag, tongs, basting brush

2 limes, zested and juiced

3 tablespoons tamari soy sauce

2 tablespoons sesame oil

1 jalapeño, seeded and cut in quarters

2 tablespoons chopped fresh ginger

3 tablespoons avocado oil

2 teaspoons honey

8 to 12 baby lamb chops

2 scallions, ends trimmed, thinly sliced, for garnish

• Place the lime zest and juice, soy sauce, sesame oil, jalapeño, ginger, avocado oil, and honey into the bowl of a food processor. Process until liquefied. Place the lamb chops into a container and pour the marinade on top and rub to coat. Cover and let the meat marinate for 4 hours or overnight.

• Preheat the grill to 550°F (290°C) or the oven to the broiler setting. Place the chops on the grill, or on a grill pan if you're cooking the chops in the oven, and cook them for 4 to 5 minutes. Turn over the chops, baste them with the marinade, and grill for another 3 to 4 minutes for medium doneness.

• Place the chops on a platter and sprinkle the scallions on top.

Fish, Vegetarian, *and* Dairy Main Dishes

PASTA SICILIANA

Dairy, Vegetarian • Serves 6 to 8

This is a dish that my husband, Andy, and I absolutely loved eating while living in Geneva, Switzerland—fried eggplant slices stirred into penne pasta with a garlicky tomato sauce and then covered in cheese and baked. Here is my healthier version using baked eggplant and whole-wheat pasta. You can use this method of baking eggplant in any recipe that calls for fried eggplant.

PREP TIME: 15 minutes • COOK TIME: 1 hour 20 minutes • ADVANCE PREP: May be made 2 days in advance and frozen • EQUIPMENT: Measuring cups and spoons, cutting board, knife, can opener, 2 jelly roll pans, offset spatula, medium saucepan, silicone spatula, wooden spoon, fork, large saucepan, colander, 9 x 13-inch (23 x 33-cm) baking dish, aluminum foil

4 tablespoons extra virgin olive oil, divided

2 large eggplants, stem and bottom trimmed, and cut into ½- to ¾-inch (12-mm to 2-cm) circles and then into ½- to ¾-inch (12-mm to 2-cm) long strips.

1 medium onion, chopped into ½-inch (12-mm) pieces

10 cloves garlic, roughly chopped

½ teaspoon dried oregano

½ teaspoon dried basil

¼ teaspoon black pepper

Pinch sugar

¼ to ½ teaspoon red pepper flakes, to taste

½ teaspoon salt

28-ounce (795-g) can crushed tomatoes

1 pound (450g) whole-wheat penne pasta

8 ounces (225g) shredded mozzarella cheese

• Preheat oven to 450°F (230°C). Place 1 tablespoon of oil on each of 2 jelly roll pans. Use an offset spatula or your hands to entirely coat each of the pans.

• Divide the eggplant slices between the 2 pans, leaving a little space between the slices. Bake the eggplant for 25 minutes. After 15 minutes, switch the pans on the racks, to ensure even browning.

• To make the sauce, place the remaining 2 tablespoons of oil into a medium saucepan and heat it over medium heat. Add the onions and cook for 5 minutes, stirring occasionally. If the onion starts to color, turn down the heat. Add the garlic and cook for 5 minutes, stirring occasionally. Add the oregano, basil, pepper, sugar, red pepper flakes, and salt, and stir. Add the crushed tomatoes and bring the mixture to a boil over medium-high heat. Reduce the heat to low. Cover the pan and simmer the sauce for 25 minutes.

• After 25 minutes of roasting, turn over the eggplant strips and roast them for another 5 to 10 minutes, until they are fork-tender and browned. Cook the pasta al dente, according to the directions on the package, and then drain it; do not overcook the pasta.

• Preheat the oven to 400°F (200°C). Place the pasta in a 9 x 13-inch (23 x 33-cm) baking dish. Add the baked eggplant slices and sauce and mix well. Cover the pan with foil and bake the eggplant for 40 minutes. Uncover the pan and sprinkle the cheese on top. Bake uncovered for another 5 minutes.

CHEESE-FILLED BUCKWHEAT BLINTZES

Dairy, Gluten-free, Vegetarian • Makes 12 blintzes

This recipe is another tribute to my grandmother Sylvia Altman, who taught me how to make crêpes (and blintzes) long before I went to cooking school in Paris. I use her cheese filling, albeit with less sugar. The recipe for the crêpes was inspired by the method used in northern France, where crêpes are made with buckwheat flour, which is rich in protein, iron, and antioxidants.

PREP TIME: 5 minutes to make batter and filling • COOK TIME: 15 minutes to cook crêpes; 8 minutes to cook blintzes in batches • ADVANCE PREP: Crêpe batter may be made 3 days in advance; filling may be made 1 day ahead; filled blintzes may be made 3 days in advance and refrigerated or frozen • EQUIPMENT: Measuring cups and spoons, Microplane zester, 3 medium bowls, whisk, sieve, fork, spoon, wax paper or parchment, 8- to 9-inch nonstick frying pan, pastry brush, silicone spatula, large plate, large frying pan

BLINTZES/CRÊPES

¾ cup (90g) buckwheat flour

1 tablespoon sugar

¼ teaspoon salt

5 teaspoons sunflower or safflower oil

1¼ cups nonfat or low-fat milk

2 large eggs

2 tablespoons (28g) unsalted butter, melted

FILLING

4 ounces (115g) cream cheese (not whipped)

7½ ounces (215g) farmer cheese

3 tablespoons sugar

1 large egg

½ teaspoon lemon zest (from 1 lemon)

¼ teaspoon pure vanilla extract

1 tablespoon sunflower oil

1 to 2 tablespoons (14 to 28g) unsalted butter

• To make the crêpes, place the buckwheat flour, sugar, salt, oil, milk, eggs, and melted butter into a medium bowl and whisk vigorously. In another bowl, strain the mixture through a sieve, pressing through as much batter as possible and then discarding the solids that remain in the sieve. The batter may be made 3 days in advance.

• To prepare the filling, place the cream cheese in a medium bowl and use a fork to mash and soften it. Add the farmer cheese and mash it into the cream cheese. Add the sugar and egg and use a spoon to mix it well. Add the lemon zest and vanilla and mix it well. The filling can be made 1 day in advance and stored covered in the fridge.

• Tear wax paper or parchment into twelve 8-inch (20-cm) pieces. Heat an 8- to 9-inch (20- to 23-cm) nonstick frying pan over medium-high heat. Brush it with a little butter. Lift the pan off the heat, scoop up a little less than ¼ cup (60ml) of the batter and pour it into the pan, just above the center, and then turn the pan clockwise 2 to 3 times, swirling the batter in order to cover the bottom of the pan, without getting any of the batter up the sides of the pan. Add more batter to cover any holes. Return the pan to the burner. By the third crêpe, you will know exactly how much batter you need.

• Cook for 45 seconds to 1 minute, and when the edges are brown, slide a silicone spatula under the crêpe to lift it up and turn it over. Cook for another 15 seconds, and then turn it onto a plate. Repeat, placing a piece of wax paper between each crêpe.

• To fill the crêpes, place one in front of you with the browner side facing up. Place 2½ tablespoons of cheese filling just above the center and spread it about 3 inches (7.5cm) wide. Fold the top down to mostly cover the filling. Fold the right and left sides 1 to 2 inches (2.5 to 5cm) toward the center, then rolling up. Set aside. You can freeze the blintzes at this point and cook them later. You do not need to thaw before cooking them, but they might take a little longer to cook.

• To cook, heat the oil and 1 tablespoon (14g) butter in a large frying pan over medium heat. Add the blintzes and cook for about 2 minutes per side or until browned, adding more butter to the pan if needed. Turn the heat down for the second batch if you are frying the blintzes in batches. Serve hot.

FISH TACOS WITH CILANTRO LIME RICE

Dairy, Fish, Gluten-free (if using corn tortillas) • Serves 6

Once you taste these tacos with baked fish, you will never go back to fried fish in a taco! As an accompaniment, Mango Coleslaw on page 7 is a must—it is easy to make and does a great job of spicing up the tacos.

PREP TIME: 10 minutes • COOK TIME: Rice: 41 minutes; fish: 10 minutes • ADVANCE PREP: Fish and rice may be made 2 days in advance • EQUIPMENT: Measuring cups and spoons, garlic press, Microplane zester, small bowl, cutting board, knife, plate, plastic wrap, small saucepan, silicone spatula, jelly roll pan, large bowl, fork

FISH

4 teaspoons ground cumin

1 tablespoon paprika

2 teaspoons garlic powder

¼ teaspoon salt

¼ teaspoon black pepper, or more to taste

2 pounds (1kg) tilapia or other white fish fillets

2 tablespoons sunflower or safflower oil

RICE

2 teaspoons sunflower or safflower oil

3 cloves garlic, crushed

1½ cups (285g) brown rice

3½ cups (840ml) boiling water

Zest of 1 lime, about 2 teaspoons

1 cup (40g) loosely packed cilantro leaves, chopped

Pinch cayenne pepper

½ teaspoon salt, or more to taste

GARNISH

Whole-wheat or corn tortillas

Guacamole from 3 avocadoes

½ cup (50g) or more shredded Mexican cheese

• To make the fish, combine the cumin, paprika, garlic powder, salt, and pepper in a small bowl. Slice the fish into strips, about 1½ inches wide (4cm) and 3 to 4 inches (7.5 to 10cm) long; I usually cut the fillets on an angle. Rub the spice mix all over the fish and put it on a plate. Cover the plate with plastic wrap and let it sit at room termperature for 30 minutes while you start the rice.

• To make the rice, heat the 2 teaspoons of oil in a small saucepan over medium heat. Add the garlic and cook it for a minute or so, stirring often, or until the garlic starts to color. Add the rice and cook it, stirring often, for another minute. Add the water, turn the heat up to medium-high, and cook the rice, uncovered, for 10 minutes. Reduce the heat to low and cook covered for another 30 minutes, or until all the water is absorbed. Let the rice sit, covered.

• Preheat the oven to broil and place a rack just above the middle of the oven. Place 2 tablespoons of oil on a jelly roll pan or other roasting pan with sides, spread to coat, and place the fish strips on top, making sure there is space between them. Place the fish in the oven and broil it for 10 minutes. The fish may be made 2 days in advance.

• Transfer the rice to a large bowl and fluff it with a fork. Add the lime zest, cilantro, cayenne, and salt and mix well. The rice may be made 2 days in advance.

• To assemble a taco, fill a tortilla with several fish slices and rice, then top with Mango Coleslaw (see page 7), guacamole, and cheese.

SPICED FISH WITH CAULIFLOWER PURÉE AND RED PEPPER TOMATO RELISH

Dairy, Fish • Serves 6

Sometimes you want to present a main course that looks like it came straight out of a restaurant kitchen, without putting in all the work to make it look that way. This recipe has three parts, but each is simple, and you can easily make the purée or relish a day or two in advance. The cauliflower purée and relish can also be served with any grilled or roasted fish or meat.

PREP TIME: 10 minutes • COOK TIME: 20 to 25 minutes for cauliflower purée; 10 minutes for relish; 20 to 25 minutes for fish • ADVANCE PREP: Purée may be made 2 days in advance, relish may be made 3days in advance; fish is best made and served the same day • EQUIPMENT: Cutting board, knife, measuring cups and spoons, medium saucepan, colander, food processor, silicone spatula or wooden spoon, large ovenproof frying pan or roasting pan

CAULIFLOWER PURÉE

1 head cauliflower, cut into florets

2 teaspoons avocado oil

½ medium onion, sliced

4 cloves garlic, roughly chopped

2 tablespoons almond milk, soy milk, or
   regular milk

¼ teaspoon salt, or more to taste

White pepper to taste

RED PEPPER TOMATO RELISH

1 tablespoon avocado oil

1 cup (110g) chopped red onions

4 cloves garlic, roughly chopped

½ red bell pepper, cut into ½-inch (12-mm) pieces

1 teaspoon sugar

1½ teaspoons apple cider vinegar

¼ cup (40g) pitted black olives, halved

8 cherry tomatoes, quartered

¼ teaspoon salt

¼ teaspoon Aleppo pepper

Black pepper to taste

FISH

2 teaspoons avocado oil

1 tablespoon ras el hanout spice mix

2-pound (1kg) halibut, cod, flounder, or other
   white fish fillet, cut into 1½-inch (4-cm)
   serving pieces, about 5½ ounces (160g) each

Ras el Hanout

This is a spice blend from North Africa that contains cinnamon, cardamom, cloves, cumin, nutmeg, mace, allspice, pepper, ginger, fenugreek, and turmeric. It is usually more flavorful than spicy.

• Fill a medium saucepan with 8 cups (2L) of water and bring to a boil. Add the cauliflower and cook until fork-tender. Drain and reserve ½ cup (120ml) cooking liquid for the sauce. May be made 2 days in advance.

• To make the cauliflower sauce, heat the avocado oil in a medium saucepan and add the onions and garlic. Cook over medium-low heat until soft, about 15 minutes. Place the cooked cauliflower, onions, and garlic into the bowl of a food processor and purée, stopping to scrape down the bowl a few times. Add the reserved cauliflower cooking liquid and milk to the bowl, and purée until

completely smooth. Add salt and white pepper to taste. Set aside. May be made 2 days in advance.

• To make the relish, heat a medium saucepan over medium heat and add the oil. Add the onions, garlic, and pepper and cook for 5 minutes, stirring often until the veggies are soft and starting to brown. Add the sugar and vinegar and cook for 1 minute. Add the olives and tomatoes and cook for another 3 minutes. Add salt, Aleppo pepper, and black pepper to the mixture. May be made 3 days in advance and reheated to serve.

• To cook the fish, preheat the oven to 350°F (180°C). Heat a large frying pan, preferably an ovenproof one, over high heat and add the avocado oil. Rub the fish filets with the ras el hanout spice mix on all sides.

• Add the fish and cook it for 5 minutes per side. If you're using an ovenproof pan, place the pan directly into the oven. If not, transfer the fish to a roasting pan. Cook the fish for another 10 to 15 minutes, or until it's done.

• To serve, reheat the purée and spoon some on the dinner plates. Place a fish fillet on top of each and top it with some relish.

KOREAN BIBIMBAP WITH TOFU

Parve, Gluten-free, Vegetarian • Serves 6

When I first prepared this recipe, I had honestly never even tasted it before. I had heard of it and seen recipes in food magazines hailing it as part of a new food trend. The key to the dish is gochujang paste, which I could not find with kosher certification when I was developing this recipe (now it can be found online, see page 143). This just meant that I had to make it from scratch. I found kosher Korean chili flakes on the Spice Jungle website. We all loved it, but whether a Korean person would say it was truly authentic, I couldn't say. All I know for sure is that these rice bowls with vegetables, tofu, and egg make a delicious meal that is fun to eat. If you have extra sauce left over, you can enjoy it on meat, chicken, or rice anytime. You could also use another kosher hot chili sauce in place of the first six ingredients.

PREP TIME: 20 minutes • COOK TIME: 5 minutes for sauce, 40 minutes for tofu and rice, 7 minutes for garnishes, 5 minutes for frying eggs in batches • ADVANCE PREP: Sauce may be made 5 days in advance; tofu may be made 3 days in advance, rice may be made 1 day in advance, garnishes should be prepared day of serving • EQUIPMENT: Measuring cups and spoons, cutting board, knife, vegetable peeler, Microplane zester, garlic press, medium saucepan, small saucepan, silicone spatula or wooden spoon, small bowl, medium bowl, whisk, paper towels, jelly roll pan, tongs, large frying pan

GOCHUJANG PASTE

2 tablespoons plus 1 teaspoon rice vinegar, divided

1 tablespoon light brown sugar

5 tablespoons water

2 tablespoons Korean red chili flakes, or other red chili powder

¼ teaspoon salt

¼ cup (70g) dark miso paste

SAUCE

4 scallions, ends trimmed, sliced

4 tablespoons tamari soy sauce

3 teaspoons sugar

2 teaspoons peeled and grated fresh ginger root

¾ teaspoon cayenne pepper

2 teaspoons sesame oil

4 teaspoons sesame seeds

4 cloves garlic, crushed

2 teaspoons honey

1 tablespoon mirin

TOFU

2 teaspoons sunflower or safflower oil

21 ounces (1½ packages [595g]) extra-firm tofu

1 tablespoon sesame oil

¼ cup (60ml) tamari soy sauce

SPINACH

2 teaspoons sunflower or safflower oil

2 large cloves garlic, crushed

10 ounces (280g) baby spinach leaves

½ teaspoon tamari soy sauce

1 teaspoon sesame oil

½ teaspoon sesame seeds

Salt and black pepper to taste

MUSHROOMS

2 tablespoons sunflower or safflower oil

8 ounces (225g) shiitake mushrooms, sliced

ADDITIONAL GARNISH

2 cups (380g) brown rice, cooked according to
   package directions

2 large carrots, peeled and shredded

2 Persian cucumbers (or ½ English cucumber), cut
   into matchsticks

1 cup (100g) shredded red cabbage

Oil or cooking spray for cooking eggs

6 large eggs

• To make the gochujang paste, place the vinegar,
brown sugar, water, chili flakes, and salt in a small
saucepan. Bring the mixture to a boil over medium
heat and then simmer it uncovered over low heat for
2 minutes, Transfer the paste to a small bowl, add
the miso paste and mix to combine, and let cool for
10 minutes.

• To prepare the sauce, place the cooled cooked paste,
scallions, soy sauce, sugar, ginger, cayenne, sesame oil,
sesame seeds, garlic, honey, and mirin into a medium
bowl and whisk it well. May be made 5 days in
advance and stored in the fridge.

• To prepare the tofu, preheat the oven to 400°F
(200°C). Drain the tofu well on paper towels. Press
more paper towels on top of the tofu to squeeze out
the last of the moisture. Slice the large block of tofu
into 10 rectangular pieces and then the smaller block
into 5 pieces. Dry the pieces with more paper towels.

Spread 2 teaspoons of oil on a jelly roll pan to cover
it completely. Place the tofu pieces in the pan in one
layer and bake it for 20 minutes.

• Meanwhile, cook the brown rice according to
package directions.

• Mix together the soy sauce and sesame oil. After the
tofu has baked for 20 minutes, pour the soy sauce and
sesame oil mixture over it. Bake for 10 minutes. Turn
the pieces over and bake for another 10 minutes.

• While the tofu bakes, prepare the spinach. Heat
sunflower oil in a large frying pan and add the garlic.
Cook for 1 minute. Add the spinach leaves, soy sauce,
and sesame oil and use tongs to toss and cook the
spinach for 1 to 2 minutes, just until it is wilted. Add
sesame seeds and salt and pepper and then place into a
bowl and set aside. Do not clean the pan.

• To prepare the mushrooms, heat the oil in the same
frying pan you just used for the spinach and cook
the mushrooms for 4 minutes on medium-high heat,
stirring them often. Set them aside.

• When everything is ready, reheat the tofu, rice,
spinach, and mushrooms, if needed. Divide the
rice among the 6 serving bowls. Add some carrots,
cucumbers, mushrooms, spinach, cabbage, and tofu
to each bowl. Heat a little oil in the frying pan and
cook the eggs sunny side up to your taste (although
you do want the yolk to remain a little soft). Divide
the eggs among the bowls and drizzle the sauce over
everything. Keep the sauce nearby, as you might want
to add more later as you dig into your bowl. I like to
mix all the components together.

DRY-RUBBED ROASTED SALMON

Fish, Gluten-free, Passover (omit seeds not available for Passover) • Serves 6

This recipe started out as one thing and then turned into something else. My plan was to coat fresh salmon with the spices that are used to cure pastrami. I rubbed my spice mix on the fish and even then I noticed that it was not very black and pastrami-like. After letting the rub sit on the salmon for a while, I simply baked it in the oven. It was only when it was done, and I'd taken it out of the oven, that I realized I'd never added any oil to the fish or the pan! I served it anyway and it was flavorful and moist, without any fat, other than what was naturally in the fish. Feel free to add more black peppercorns to the spice mix if you want more kick.

PREP TIME: 5 minutes to make spice mix; marinate for 30 minutes • COOK TIME: 20 to 22 minutes • ADVANCE PREP: Spice mix may be made 1 week in advance; fish may be cooked 1 day in advance • EQUIPMENT: Measuring spoons, cutting board, knife, jelly roll pan, coffee grinder or food processor (or mortar and pestle, or quart resealable plastic bag and rolling pin), small bowl, spoon large plate

3-pound (1.5-kg) salmon fillet, whole or
   cut into 6 8-ounce (250-g) servings

1 tablespoon coriander seeds

1 tablespoon whole black peppercorns,
   or more to taste

1 tablespoon black or yellow mustard seeds

2 teaspoons juniper berries

1 teaspoon fennel seeds

2 teaspoons light brown sugar

2 teaspoons garlic powder

1 teaspoon onion powder

½ teaspoon smoked or regular paprika

¼ teaspoon ground cloves

½ teaspoon kosher salt

• Place the coriander seeds, black peppercorns, mustard seeds, juniper berries, and fennel seeds into a coffee grinder or food processor and grind them into small pieces (making sure none are left whole), but not completely into a powder. If you use a food processor and some of the spices are still too big after processing, crush them using a mortar and pestle, or put them in a quart resealable plastic bag and then smash it with a rolling pin. Transfer the ground seeds, peppercorns, and the rest of the mixture into a small bowl. Add the brown sugar, garlic powder, onion powder, paprika, cloves, and salt, and mix well.

• Spread the spice mix on a plate and press each slice of salmon into the mix to cover it completely. Use all the spice mix. Place the fish on a roasting pan, leaving space between the pieces. Let the fish sit at room temperature for 30 minutes, covered with plastic wrap, or refrigerate it if you will be cooking it later.

• Preheat oven to 400°F (200°C). Bake the salmon for 20 to 22 minutes, 20 minutes if you like it a little pink inside, longer if you want it fully cooked. Serve the fish hot or at room temperature.

DAL CURRY

Parve, Vegan or Vegetarian, Gluten-free • Serves 12

This is the main dish to make when you have a vegan or vegetarian at your Shabbat or holiday table, although everyone will want to try it. When I make it to serve on weeknights, I like preparing it early in the week so I have it available to eat all week long. The curry leaves will definitely improve the taste, but if you can't find them at the store, the dish is also very good without them.

PREP TIME: Soak split peas for 8 hours or overnight; 20 minutes • COOK TIME: 1 hour 25 minutes • ADVANCE PREP: May be made 3 days in advance • EQUIPMENT: Measuring cups and spoons, cutting board, knife, large bowl, colander, large saucepan or Dutch oven, silicone spatula or wooden spoon, medium frying pan

2 cups (300g) yellow split peas

6 cups (1.4L) water

3 medium tomatoes, cut into 1½ inch (4-cm) pieces

1 teaspoon garlic powder

1 teaspoon ground cumin

1 teaspoon ground turmeric

3 medium onions, finely chopped, divided

1½ large jalapeños, seeded and chopped, divided

1 teaspoon salt, or more to taste

1 bunch cilantro leaves, chopped, and more for garnish, if desired

2 teaspoons sunflower or safflower oil

½ teaspoon yellow mustard seeds

12 fresh curry leaves, found in an Indian market

3 dried red chilies, crushed or chopped

• Place the split peas and 6 cups (1.4L) water into a large bowl and let soak for 8 hours or overnight. Drain.

• Place the drained split peas and water into a large saucepan or Dutch oven and bring to a boil. Skim off any dirty-looking foam. Cook, uncovered, over low heat for 45 minutes to 1 hour, or until the peas are soft. Stir often.

• Add the tomatoes, garlic powder, cumin, turmeric, 2 onions, 1 jalapeño, and ½ teaspoon salt. Cook for another 30 minutes, or until creamy, and the split peas are very soft, stirring often. Add the cilantro leaves and another ½ teaspoon salt to taste.

• In a medium frying pan, heat the oil over medium heat. Add the remaining ½ jalapeño to the pan. Add the remaining onions to the pan and cook for 5 minutes. Add the mustard seeds, curry leaves, and red chilies and stir. Cook until well browned, about 10 minutes. Add to the split pea mixture and stir. Cook for another 5 minutes. Add salt to taste. If the mixture gets too thick, add ½ cup (120ml) water, or more, if needed.

BLACK BEAN CHILI

Parve, Vegan or Vegetarian • Serves 6

This is a Shoyer family staple, and we probably have burritos once a week using this easy chili recipe. I serve these beans with rice, tortillas, cheese, and guacamole often made by my son Jake. I have taught this recipe to teens at Camp Ramah New England for ten years as a basic recipe that can be made with any type of bean. I consider this a dish that every child should know how to make before leaving home. Should be served with Cilantro Lime Rice (page 68) and the Mango Coleslaw (page 7).

PREP TIME: 10 minutes • COOK TIME: 30 minutes • ADVANCE PREP: May be made 3 days in advance • EQUIPMENT: Measuring cups and spoons, cutting board, knife, garlic press, can opener, medium saucepan, silicone spatula or wooden spoon

2 tablespoons sunflower, safflower, or canola oil

1 small onion, peeled and chopped into ¼-inch (6-mm) pieces

3 cloves garlic, peeled and minced

½ teaspoon ground cumin

½ teaspoon paprika

Salt and black pepper to taste

1 medium tomato, seeded and chopped

½ cup (120ml) tomato sauce

1 26.5-ounce (750g) can black beans, drained and rinsed with water

• Heat the oil in a medium saucepan. Add the onions and garlic and cook for 5 minutes, stirring a few times. Add the cumin, paprika, and salt and pepper. Cook for 3 minutes.

• Add the tomato and tomato sauce and cook for another 2 minutes. Add the beans and bring to a boil. Reduce heat to low, cover, and simmer on low heat for 20 minutes. Serve hot with tortillas, cilantro lime rice, mango coleslaw, cheese, and guacamole, as you like.

> ### Planning Meals for Children and Teens
>
> Meals such as make-your-own burritos have been very popular with my four children. I believe the appeal is that everyone can assemble the burrito as they like. Use this approach for other meals: rice or noodle bowls with chicken, fish, or meat and an assortment of raw and cooked vegetables to add on top, plus sauces. It allows kids to control their meal and have ownership over what is on their plate. I think it makes a meal more fun to have choices and inspires children to eat more and better.

RED QUINOA MEATBALLS WITH SPAGHETTI SQUASH

Parve, Gluten-free, Vegetarian, Passover (use quinoa flour or potato starch)

• Serves 4 to 6 (makes 12 meatballs)

This recipe is one of my favorites in this book. I learned from recipe testers Howard and Trudy Jacobson that it is even low in Weight Watchers points. These meatballs won over friends who don't even like quinoa. You really feel like you are eating classic spaghetti and meatballs, one of my favorite dishes that my mother made often. You can even sprinkle cheese on top of these "meat"balls. You can also prepare the spaghetti squash and sauce as a side dish with another main.

PREP TIME: 15 minutes; chill firmed meatballs for 1 hour • COOK TIME: Squash cooks for 45 to 50 minutes; quinoa cooks for 15 minutes; sauce cooks for 25 minutes; meatballs cook for 35 to 40 minutes • ADVANCE PREP: Any components may be made 2 days in advance • EQUIPMENT: Cutting board, knife, measuring cups and spoons, garlic press, can opener, jelly roll pan, fork, 2 large bowls, small saucepan, medium frying pan, silicone spatula or wooden spoon, small bowl, plate, medium saucepan, tongs, ladle

SPAGHETTI SQUASH

1 large spaghetti squash, sliced in half the long way, seeded

1 tablespoon extra virgin olive oil

QUINOA MEATBALLS

¾ cup (130g) red quinoa

1½ cups (360ml) water

2 tablespoons plus 1 teaspoon extra virgin olive oil, divided

1 onion, finely chopped

3 cloves garlic, crushed

½ teaspoon dried basil

½ teaspoon dried oregano

2 large eggs

2 tablespoons quinoa flour (or chickpea flour or potato starch)

4 teaspoons finely chopped fresh Italian parsley

⅛ teaspoon salt

¼ teaspoon black pepper

TOMATO SAUCE

2 tablespoons extra virgin olive oil

1 medium onion, chopped

8 cloves garlic, chopped

¼ teaspoon dried basil

¼ teaspoon dried oregano

¼ teaspoon salt or more to taste

¼ teaspoon black pepper

Pinch sugar

1 28-ounce (795-g) can crushed tomatoes

½ cup (120ml) water

• To make the spaghetti squash, preheat the oven to 375°F (190°C). Drizzle squash halves with oil and place the cut side down on a jelly roll pan. Bake the squash for 45 to 50 minutes, or until it is fork-tender. Let cool. Use a fork to scrape the squash into a large bowl. Set aside until you're ready to serve.

• To make the meatballs, place the quinoa and water in a small saucepan and bring it to a boil over high heat. Cover the pan, reduce the heat to low, and simmer for 15 minutes, or until all of the water has been absorbed. Let the quinoa cool 15 minutes.

• While the quinoa is cooking, heat 2 tablespoons of oil in a medium frying pan over medium-low heat. Add the onions and cook for 5 to 7 minutes, or until soft and starting to brown. Add the garlic and the remaining teaspoon of oil to the pan and cook for another 3 minutes. Transfer to a large bowl and let cool for 10 minutes.

• Add the cooled quinoa to the bowl with the onions and garlic. Add the basil, oregano, eggs, quinoa flour, and parsley and mix well. Add salt and pepper and mix well.

• Pour some water into a small bowl. Dip your hands in the water and then scoop up about 3 tablespoons of the quinoa mixture and shape into a ball. Press the ball tightly and put it on a plate. Wet your hands before shaping each meatball. Chill the meatballs in the fridge for at least 1 hour and up to overnight.

• To make the sauce, heat the oil in a medium saucepan over medium heat. Add onions and cook for 5 minutes. Add the garlic and cook for another 5 minutes. Add the basil, oregano, salt, pepper, and sugar and stir. Add the tomatoes and water and bring the mixture to a boil. Reduce the heat to low and simmer the sauce, covered, for 25 minutes.

• Preheat the oven to 400°F (200°C). Put 2 tablespoons of olive oil onto a jelly roll pan and heat in the oven for 2 to 3 minutes. Carefully place the meatballs on the hot pan and bake for 25 to 30 minutes, or until firm.

• To serve, reheat the squash and sauce. Using tongs, place some squash on a plate, ladle some sauce over it, then add the meatballs and more sauce, if desired.

FRITTATA WITH ZUCCHINI, CARAMELIZED ONIONS, AND HERBS

Dairy, Gluten-free, Vegetarian, Passover • Serves 4 to 6

A frittata is how you make an omelet for a crowd. You can use any herbs you like in this recipe.

PREP TIME: 20 minutes • COOK TIME: 23 minutes • ADVANCE PREP: May be made 2 days in advance • EQUIPMENT: Measuring cups and spoons, cutting board, knife, garlic press, large ovenproof frying pan, silicone spatula, plate small bowl, fork, large bowl, whisk,

3 tablespoons extra virgin olive oil, divided

1 leek, white part only, halved and sliced

1 large onion, chopped into ½-inch (12-mm) pieces, about 1½ cups

3 cloves garlic, crushed

1 medium to large zucchini, unpeeled, cut into 1-inch (2.5-cm) pieces, about 2½ cups

½ teaspoon salt, divided

10 large eggs plus 1 egg white

½ cup (120ml) milk

¼ teaspoon black pepper

3 tablespoons chopped herbs: dill, Italian parsley, basil, cilantro, etc.

• Preheat the oven to 350°F (180°C). Heat 2 tablespoons of the oil in a large ovenproof frying pan over medium heat. Add the leeks and onions and cook for 10 minutes, stirring often until lightly browned. Add the garlic and cook for another minute. Transfer the mixture to a plate or small bowl.

• Add the remaining tablespoon of oil to the pan and add the zucchini cubes. Cook them for 5 minutes, letting the cubes sit for a full minute at first before stirring, then cook, stirring just a few times, until the zucchini is fork-tender. Add ¼ teaspoon of salt to the mix and stir. Return the leeks, onions, and garlic to the pan and mix well.

• While the vegetables are cooking, place the eggs, egg white, milk, remaining ¼ teaspoon salt, pepper, and herbs in a large bowl and whisk them thoroughly. Pour the mixture into the pan and cook it over medium-low heat. Cook it, uncovered, until the edges start to set, for about 3 minutes. Place the pan, uncovered, into the oven and bake for 15 to 17 minutes, or until it has set.

• Run a silicone spatula around the edges of the frittata and flip it onto a serving plate. Serve warm.

Side Dishes

CHOPPED STRING BEANS WITH BASIL AND PINE NUTS

Parve, Gluten-free, Vegan • Serves 6 to 8

Use haricots verts, thin French string beans, if you can find them. I like to make this recipe when I am making many different dishes for a meal because the chopped haricots verts take up less room on the dinner plate than regular length green beans.

PREP TIME: 10 minutes • COOK TIME: 15 minutes • ADVANCE PREP: May be made 2 days in advance • EQUIPMENT: Measuring cups and spoons, cutting board, knife, large frying pan and lid, silicone spatula, small bowl

½ cup (70g) pine nuts

2 tablespoons extra virgin olive oil

6 cloves garlic, finely chopped

1½ pounds (680g) haricots verts, or regular string beans, trimmed and chopped into ¾-inch (2-cm) pieces

1 tablespoon water, if using haricots verts, and 2 tablespoons of water, if using regular string beans

¼ teaspoon salt, or more to taste

¼ teaspoon black pepper

1 cup (40g) basil leaves, sliced chiffonade (stacked in piles and then thinly sliced)

• Heat a large frying pan over medium-high heat. Add the pine nuts and cook, stirring often, until lightly browned and releasing their aroma. Transfer the pine nuts to a small bowl and set them aside. May be made 1 day in advance.

• Heat the olive oil in the same pan over medium heat. Add the garlic and sauté it for 1 minute, stirring a few times. Turn the heat up to medium-high, add the beans, and cook for 5 minutes, stirring often. Add the water and cook the beans, covered, for another 4 minutes. If they are still not fork-tender, cook for another 2 to 3 minutes. Add salt and pepper and remove the pan from the heat.

• When you're ready to serve, reheat the beans and add the basil and pine nuts. Add more salt and pepper if desired.

EGGPLANT WITH CAPERS AND MINT

Parve, Gluten-free, Vegan, Passover • Serves 4 to 6

This is a very simple recipe that looks impressive. I prefer to broil the eggplant in the oven, but you can also grill it outdoors. When I broil eggplant in the oven, I cover the pan with heavy-duty aluminum foil to make cleanup easier.

PREP TIME: 5 minutes • COOK TIME: 10 minutes • ADVANCE PREP: May be made 2 days in advance •
EQUIPMENT: Measuring cups and spoons, cutting board, knife, broiler pan, pastry brush, tongs, fork, small bowl

3 tablespoons extra virgin olive oil, divided

1 large eggplant, unpeeled, cut into ¾-inch (2-cm) round slices

¼ cup (35g) finely chopped red onions

¼ cup (30g) capers, drained

¼ teaspoon salt

¼ teaspoon black pepper

Kosher salt to sprinkle on top

¼ cup (13g) mint leaves, about 10 large, chopped into small pieces

---

To Salt or Not to Salt Eggplant

Years ago, when recipes instructed me to salt eggplant slices for 45 minutes and rinse before cooking, I dutifully complied. As I got busier cooking for a larger family and entertaining more, I ignored this step because it took too much time. I found that it did not make a difference in the taste of my eggplant recipes. In short, no need to salt the eggplant before cooking.

• If you're making the eggplant in the oven, preheat oven to broil. Pour 1 tablespoon of the olive oil on a broiler pan or other baking pan and brush it on. Add the eggplant slices in one layer and brush them with another tablespoon of oil. Broil the eggplant for 5 minutes, or until the slices are browned. Using tongs or a fork, turn over the eggplant slices and broil them for another 4 to 5 minutes. Let the eggplant cool for 3 minutes and then place the slices on a serving platter. If you're making the eggplant on an outdoor gas grill, preheat the grill to 550°F (290°C). Brush the eggplant with oil and grill it for a few minutes until browned, and then turn it over and grill until fork-tender.

• In a small bowl, place the chopped red onions, capers, and remaining tablespoon of olive oil, salt, and pepper and mix. Sprinkle the mixture over the eggplant slices. Add some kosher salt on top. Sprinkle the mint all over the eggplant. Serve at room temperature.

ROASTED BROCCOLI WITH MUSTARD AND ZA'ATAR DRIZZLE

Parve, Gluten-free, Vegan • Serves 4 to 5

This preparation can also be done with cauliflower and is easily doubled to serve more people. It is a great side for a barbecue, as it can be prepared earlier in the day and served at room temperature. The recipe calls for pink peppercorns, which are soft and easily crushed. Do not substitute black or white whole peppercorns, as they are too hard for this dish.

PREP TIME: 5 minutes • COOK TIME: 20 to 25 minutes • ADVANCE PREP: May be made 2 days in advance • EQUIPMENT: Cutting board, knife, measuring cups and spoons, cookie sheet or jelly roll pan, fork, small bowl, whisk

1 head broccoli (about 1 pound [450g]), trimmed and cut into florets, stems cut into chunks

2 tablespoons extra virgin olive oil, divided

1 teaspoon water

2 teaspoons Dijon mustard

1 teaspoon za'atar

Pinch chili powder

Salt and black pepper, to taste

1 teaspoon pink peppercorns

• Heat the oven to 400°F (200°C). Place the broccoli pieces on a cookie sheet or jelly roll pan, drizzle with 1 tablespoon of the oil and toss to coat. Roast in the oven for 20 to 25 minutes, or until fork-tender.

• Meanwhile, in a small bowl, whisk together the remaining tablespoon of oil, water, mustard, za'atar, chili powder, salt, and pepper. Whisk well.

• When the broccoli is cooked, remove it from the oven and place it on a serving platter. Drizzle the broccoli with the za'atar dressing and then crush the pink peppercorns in your fingers and sprinkle them on top. Serve the broccoli warm or at room temperature.

CHARRED CAULIFLOWER WITH ORANGE VINAIGRETTE

Gluten-free, Vegan, Passover • Serves 4 to 6

This recipe tastes best when the cauliflower is cooked on an outdoor grill and becomes charred and black. If you broil the cauliflower in the oven, make sure that the pieces get some black char marks to give the dish the grilled flavor that makes it so unique.

PREP TIME: 5 minutes • COOK TIME: 12 to 14 minutes • ADVANCE PREP: May be made 2 days in advance • EQUIPMENT: Measuring cups and spoons, Microplane zester, citrus juicer, garlic press, cutting board, knife, jelly roll pan, small bowl, tongs, whisk

1 large head cauliflower

3 to 5 tablespoons extra virgin olive oil, divided

1 teaspoon orange zest (from 1 orange)

1 tablespoon fresh orange juice, from zested orange

1 large clove garlic, crushed

1 tablespoon water

Salt and black pepper to taste

8 large basil leaves, rolled up the long way and sliced into ribbons (chiffonade)

• If you are using the oven, pour 1 tablespoon of oil on a jelly roll pan and spread to coat.

• Turn on the grill or preheat the oven to broil with a rack placed in the top third of the oven. Remove the outer green leaves from the head of the cauliflower. Rinse the cauliflower well and trim off any dirty spots. Trim the bottom and place the cauliflower on a cutting board, stem side down. Using a long sharp knife, slice the head in half from the stem to the top of the head. Cut ¾-inch (2-cm) slices and place them, one at a time, in one layer on a shallow serving platter—or the jelly roll pan, if you're cooking them in the oven. Some of the slices may crumble into smaller pieces. Place any 1-inch (2.5-cm) or larger pieces of cauliflower on the platter or pan with the slices.

• Measure about 1 tablespoon of the really tiny cauliflower pieces, chop them finely, and set them aside in a small bowl.

• Drizzle the cauliflower slices with 1 to 2 tablespoons of olive oil. When the grill is at 550°F (290°C), add the slices and cook for 6 minutes. Using tongs, turn them over and cook for another 2 minutes, until charred and the thicker pieces are just fork-tender. If you're cooking the cauliflower in the oven, broil the slices until very well browned, about 7 minutes per side. Place the grilled cauliflower back on the platter in one layer.

• Add the remaining 2 tablespoons of oil, orange zest, orange juice, garlic, and water to the cauliflower pieces in the bowl and whisk well. Drizzle the mixture over the cauliflower pieces, add salt and pepper to taste, and scatter the basil leaves on top. Serve at room temperature.

Slivering Basil

Stack basil leaves and then roll them up the long way. Cut across the rolls to create thin slices. This is also called "chiffonade."

PEAS AND CARROTS REINVENTED: GRILLED WHOLE CARROTS WITH ENGLISH PEA DIP

Gluten-free, Vegan • Serves 6

Like many of you who grew up in the late 1960s and 1970s, most of the vegetables I ate came from a can. One of the classics was a peas-and-carrots combination, which was both extremely soft and light on flavor. Yet, every time I pass those cans in the supermarket, I smile with nostalgia. I think the only canned vegetable I ever bought as an adult was canned corn, when my kids were younger. So here is my grown-up ode to the classic combo—grilled whole carrots with a purée of frozen peas and tarragon.

PREP TIME: 5 minutes • COOK TIME: 10 to 12 minutes for carrots; 18 minutes for pea purée • ADVANCE PREP: May be made 2 days in advance • EQUIPMENT: Vegetable brush, measuring cups and spoons, cutting board, knife, tongs, fork, small saucepan with lid, silicone spatula or wooden spoon, immersion blender or food processor

2 pounds (1 kg) carrots, scrubbed clean and unpeeled

2 tablespoons sunflower or safflower oil

1 medium onion, chopped into 1-inch (2.5-cm) pieces

3 cloves garlic, chopped roughly

1½ cups (200g) frozen peas

½ cup (120ml) water

1 tablespoon fresh tarragon leaves

¼ teaspoon salt, plus more to taste to sprinkle on carrots, if desired

⅛ teaspoon white pepper

• Preheat the outdoor gas grill to medium-high, so the heat stays at 550°F (290°C). Rub the carrots with 1 tablespoon of the oil. Grill the carrots for a total of 10 to 12 minutes, turning them often with tongs, until charred on all sides and fork-tender. Make sure the carrots hold their shape and do not get too soft.

• Meanwhile, heat the remaining 1 tablespoon of oil in a small saucepan over medium heat and cook the onions and garlic for 8 to 10 minutes, stirring often, until they start to brown. Add the peas and water. Cook the mixture, covered, for 5 to 8 minutes, or until the peas are soft. Add the tarragon leaves, salt, and white pepper, re-cover the pan, and let it sit for 5 minutes.

• Purée the pea mixture with an immersion blender, or transfer it to a food processor. Serve the puréed peas warm, alongside the carrots, as a dip. May be made 2 days in advance.

KASHA MUJADARRA

Parve, Gluten-free, Vegetarian • Serves 8

Kasha varenishkas, buckwheat groats with bowtie pasta and onions, is a must on every visit to a New York kosher deli. It turns out that buckwheat has magical powers—it reduces the risks of diabetes and heart disease. Not only that, but I was shocked to learn that buckwheat is not even a wheat, but a fruit seed, and is gluten-free! So when your *bubbe* offers you kasha, say yes, but ask her to try my recipe with fiber-rich lentils and lots of onions, plus Middle Eastern spices, making it way more interesting and moist than the deli version.

PREP TIME: 10 minutes • COOK TIME: 25 to 30 minutes • ADVANCE PREP: Kasha and lentils may each be cooked 2 days in advance; completed dish may be made 2 days in advance • EQUIPMENT: Measuring cups and spoons, cutting board, knife, garlic press, small saucepan, sieve, whisk, silicone spatula, 2 medium bowls, medium saucepan with lid, large frying pan

⅓ cup (65g) lentils

1 large egg white

¾ cup (125g) coarse kasha (buckwheat groats)

1½ cups (360ml) boiling water (have ready when you start cooking the kasha)

3 tablespoons extra virgin olive oil, divided

2 large onions, halved and chopped into ½ to ¾-inch (12-mm to 2-cm) pieces

4 cloves garlic, crushed

1 teaspoon ground turmeric

½ teaspoon ground cumin

¼ teaspoon paprika

¼ teaspoon chili pepper

½ teaspoon ground cinnamon

½ teaspoon black pepper, plus more to taste

¼ teaspoon kosher salt, plus more to taste

¼ cup (35g) pine nuts

• Place the lentils in a small saucepan with 2 cups (480ml) of water. Bring it to a boil and cook, uncovered, over medium heat (it should be bubbling) for 12 to 15 minutes, or until the lentils are al dente, done but not soft. Start tasting them after 12 minutes to see if they are done. Drain the lentils through a sieve and let them sit. May be cooked 2 days in advance and stored in the fridge.

• Meanwhile, use a whisk to beat the egg white in a medium bowl. Add the kasha kernels and whisk the mixture to coat the grains with the egg white. Heat a medium saucepan over medium-high heat. When it's hot, add the kasha and egg and cook it for 3 minutes, stirring often, to toast the kasha and break apart the clumps. Use a whisk to separate the grains, but you will also need a wooden spoon or spatula to move the grains from the sides of the saucepan to the middle so that they toast evenly. Keep stirring to toast the kasha.

• Add the boiling water, wait a few seconds so it stops splattering, and then stir and cover the pan. Turn the heat to low and cook the kasha for 10 minutes, or until most of the water has been absorbed. Use a whisk to stir the kasha, and then cover and cook it for another 2 minutes. Turn off the heat and let the kasha sit for 5 minutes. Transfer it to a medium bowl and mix the kasha to break it apart. Let it cool and dry out while you cook the onions and spices. Kasha may be cooked 2 days in advance.

• While the kasha is cooking, heat 2 tablespoons of the oil in a large frying pan over medium-high heat. Add the onions and cook for 15 to 20 minutes, stirring often, to brown completely. Reduce the heat to medium-low and add another tablespoon of oil. Add the garlic, turmeric, cumin, paprika, chili pepper, cinnamon, pepper, and salt and mix well. Cook for another 3 minutes.

• Add the kasha and mix it well. Mix in the lentils and add more salt and pepper to taste. Cook for 2 minutes, stirring the whole time. Taste and add ¼ teaspoon salt. Add more pepper, if desired. Transfer everything to a serving bowl. Wipe out the pan with paper towels. Return the pan to the stove over medium heat. Add the pine nuts and cook, stirring often until toasted, about 3 to 4 minutes. Scatter the pine nuts on top on the kasha and serve. May be made 2 days in advance.

Entertaining with Ease

When I am hosting a large crowd for Friday night or a holiday, I work very hard to prepare as much of the meal in advance as I can so I too can enjoy the gathering with my guests. Avoid dishes that must be made right before you serve them, like salads. Set the table earlier in the day. Have all your soup bowls out and ready, and prepare any soup garnishes in advance. Remove platters from the cabinet beforehand and use stickies to label which dish will go into each one.

POTATO AND SCALLION LATKES WITH PICKLED APPLESAUCE

Parve, Gluten-free, Vegetarian, Passover • Serves 6

Everyone loves potato latkes but no one likes the mess of frying them, or the guilt associated with eating them. These latkes are baked in the oven and easily won over my kids. You do need to watch them so they do not burn; they were done at different times in different ovens. The Pickled Applesauce is basically a tangy-spicy applesauce, which we also eat with schnitzel.

PREP TIME: 10 minutes • COOK TIME: 20 to 24 minutes • ADVANCE PREP: Latkes may be made 2 days in advance and reheated in the oven or frozen; applesauce may be made 4 days in advance • EQUIPMENT: Cutting board, knife, vegetable brush, measuring cups and spoons, citrus juicer, vegetable peeler, 2 jelly roll pans, food processor, medium bowl, box grater, wooden spoon, oven mitts, slotted spatula, small saucepan with lid, immersion blender

LATKES

2 tablespoons sunflower or safflower oil, or more if needed

½ medium onion, quartered

3 scallions, ends trimmed, cut into thin slices or chopped into small pieces

3 medium potatoes (about 1½ pounds [700g]), scrubbed clean and unpeeled

2 teaspoons (10ml) fresh lemon juice

2 large eggs

½ teaspoon baking powder

2 tablespoons potato starch

½ teaspoon salt

¼ teaspoon black pepper

PICKLED APPLESAUCE

1 teaspoon sunflower or safflower oil

⅓ cup red onions, chopped into ¼-inch (6-mm) pieces

2 tablespoons apple cider vinegar

2 tablespoons light brown sugar

2 apples, peeled and cut into ½-inch (12-mm) cubes

¼ teaspoon ground coriander

¼ teaspoon ground ginger

1 cinnamon stick

¼ teaspoon salt

Pinch black pepper

• To make the latkes, preheat the oven to 450°F (230°C). When the oven is hot, pour 2 tablespoons of oil onto 2 jelly roll pans and turn them in every direction so that the oil coats the pans. Heat the pans in the oven for 5 minutes.

• Place the onions and scallions in the bowl of a food processor and chop them into small pieces. Place them in a medium bowl. Shred the potatoes by hand on the large holes of a box grater or in a food processor with the shredding blade, and place in the bowl. Add the lemon juice, eggs, baking powder, potato starch, salt, and pepper and mix well.

• Very carefully (I mean really carefully; move very slowly) remove one of the pans and use your hands or a spoon to scoop up and drop clumps of the potato mixture, a little less than ¼ cup, onto the pan. I use my hands. Press the mixture down to flatten it a little.

• Place the pan in the oven for 10 to 12 minutes and immediately remove the second oiled pan. Repeat the same process with the remaining potato mixture and bake the second pan of latkes for 10 to 12 minutes. Bake them until the edges are well browned, and then with a slotted spatula turn them over and cook the latkes for another 8 to 10 minutes, or until the bottoms are browned. May be made 2 days in advance and reheated in the oven.

• Meanwhile, to make the applesauce, heat the oil in a small saucepan over medium heat. Add the onions and cook them for 3 minutes, until they soften. Add the vinegar and brown sugar and cook for another 3 minutes. Add the apples, coriander, ginger, cinnamon stick, salt, and pepper, and cook, covered, on low heat for 15 minutes, or until the apples are soft. Let the mixture cool for 10 minutes and then purée it, using an immersion blender or a food processor. May be made 4 days in advance and served warm or cold.

TZIMMIS PURÉE

Gluten-free, Vegan, Passover • Serves 10 to 12

Not to make a whole tzimmis about it (tzimmis being Yiddish for "a big fuss"), but tzimmis, a stew of sweet potatoes, carrots, and dried fruit, is becoming one of those lost and forgotten jewels of Ashkenazi cuisine. I make it every Rosh Hashanah so my children know what it is. Here is my updated version, which truly tastes like my usual tzimmis, but is presented more elegantly as a French purée. I'm planning to serve it on Thanksgiving as well.

PREP TIME: 8 minutes • COOK TIME: 32 minutes • ADVANCE PREP: May be made 2 days in advance • EQUIPMENT: Measuring cups and spoons, cutting board, knife, vegetable peeler, Microplane zester, medium saucepan, silicone spatula or wooden spoon, immersion blender or food processor

1 tablespoon sunflower or safflower oil

1 medium onion, cut into 1-inch (2.5-cm) pieces

2 cloves garlic, chopped

2 pounds (1 kg) sweet potatoes, peeled and cut into 1-inch (2.5-cm) cubes

4 carrots, peeled and cut into 1-inch (2.5-cm) chunks

1 cup (200g) dried apricots

½ teaspoon orange zest (from 1 orange)

1 cinnamon stick

2 cups (480ml) water

Salt and black pepper to taste

• Heat the oil in a medium saucepan over medium heat. Add the onions and cook them for 3 to 5 minutes, or until translucent and just starting to color. Add the garlic and cook for another 2 minutes.

• Add the sweet potatoes, carrots, apricots, orange zest, cinnamon stick, and water and bring to a boil. Stir the mixture, cover it, and cook for 20 to 25 minutes, or until the carrots and sweet potatoes are soft. Let the mixture cool for 10 minutes, covered.

• Remove the cinnamon stick and use either an immersion blender to purée the mixture until it is smooth, or transfer it to a food processor. Taste the tzimmis and add salt and pepper if desired.

White Sweet Potatoes?

When I was living in Geneva, Switzerland, in the 1990s, I celebrated Thanksgiving every year. The first year, I went to the Migros supermarket and bought sweet potatoes that looked just like the ones we had at home. I schlepped my groceries home and proceeded to peel the sweet potatoes only to discover that they were white inside. Confused, I went to another store and bought some more. After the second batch was also white inside, I gave up and continued with my side dish, which tasted great but was not orange, as planned. So if you cannot find orange sweet potatoes where you live, use butternut squash instead. I have since learned that there are 6,500 varieties of sweet potatoes with flesh that might be red-orange, yellow, orange, dark orange, cream, or white.

BRUSSELS SPROUT CRUMBS

Gluten-free, Vegan, Passover • Serves 6

Whenever I roast Brussels sprouts, I find myself picking on the crispy, chip-like leaves that fall off the bigger pieces while they're cooking. This recipe gives me an entire pan of mostly crispy pieces.

PREP TIME: 8 minutes • COOK TIME: 25 minutes • ADVANCE PREP: May be made 2 days in advance but best made and served same day if you want them crispy • EQUIPMENT: Cutting board, knife, jelly roll or baking pan, fork

2 pounds (1 kg) Brussels sprouts, cleaned and trimmed, outer leaves removed (see Tip, page 9)

2 tablespoons sunflower or safflower oil

2 teaspoons balsamic vinegar (the thicker the better)

¼ teaspoon black pepper

¼ teaspoon kosher salt

• Preheat oven to 450°F (230°C). Trim the ends off each Brussels sprout and remove the outer leaves and discard them. Trim off any bad parts. Put the Brussels sprouts in a colander and rinse them well. Dry them on a clean dishtowel. Pick up handfuls of sprouts and place them on a large cutting board. Chop the Brussels sprouts roughly so that the pieces are no larger than ¾ to 1 inch (2 to 2.5cm).

• Place all the Brussels sprouts pieces and leaves on a jelly roll pan or baking pan with sides. Add the oil, vinegar, and pepper and toss to coat. Bake the sprouts for 25 minutes, stirring once, until the larger pieces are fork-tender and the smaller pieces are very crisp.

• Remove the Brussels sprouts from the oven, sprinkle salt on top, and stir. May be made 2 days in advance but are best made just before eaten so they are crispy.

QUINOA WITH MUSHROOMS AND KALE

Gluten-free, Vegan, Passover • Serves 6 to 8

I always thought that mushrooms had little nutritional value, but I was misled. Mushrooms have minerals that reduce inflammation and improve liver function, and their fiber, vitamin C, and potassium content all contribute to heart health. This recipe uses cremini, shiitake, and dried porcini mushrooms, but you can substitute other types as well.

PREP TIME: 10 minutes • COOK TIME: 15 to 20 minutes • ADVANCE PREP: May be made 3 days in advance • EQUIPMENT: Measuring cups and spoons, cutting board, knife, garlic press, small saucepan with lid, large frying pan (with sides), silicone spatula, paper towels, medium bowl

¾ cup (130g) quinoa

3 tablespoons extra virgin olive oil, divided

1 large onion, chopped into ½-inch (12-mm) pieces

1 large shallot, halved and sliced into ¼-inch (6-mm) slices

8 to 10 ounces (225 to 280g) cremini mushrooms, bottoms trimmed, halved and sliced

8 to 10 ounces (225 to 280g) shiitake mushrooms, bottoms trimmed, halved and sliced

2 cloves garlic, crushed and divided

¼ teaspoon salt

¼ teaspoon black pepper

½ cup (10 g) dried porcini mushrooms, soaked in ½ cup (120ml) hot water for 10 minutes

2 cups (130g) chopped curly kale leaves (about 1-inch [2.5-cm] pieces)

1 to 2 teaspoons white truffle oil, to taste

• Place the quinoa and 1½ cups (360ml) water in a small saucepan and bring it to a boil over medium heat. Reduce the heat to low, cover the pan, and cook the quinoa for 15 minutes, or until the liquid has been absorbed. Set it aside.

• While the quinoa is cooking, heat 2 tablespoons of the oil in a large frying pan with sides over medium heat and cook the onions and shallots for 5 minutes, stirring occasionally. Add the cremini and shiitake mushrooms and cook them for another 5 minutes, stirring often. Add 1 clove of crushed garlic, salt, and pepper and stir. Lift the porcini mushrooms out of their soaking water and, using paper towels, squeeze out any excess liquid. Roughly chop the mushrooms, add them to the pan, and stir.

• Place the kale in a medium bowl, add the remaining tablespoon of oil and massage the oil into the leaves to soften them. Add the kale to the pan with the mushrooms and cook for 2 minutes.

• When the quinoa is cooked, add it to the pan. Add the remaining crushed clove of garlic and cook over medium heat for 2 minutes, mixing everything together. Taste and adjust seasonings if needed.

• Place the quinoa into a serving bowl, drizzle the truffle oil on top, and mix it in.

Cleaning Mushrooms

Rinse mushrooms under a light stream of water and use your fingers to wipe off any dirt. Dry the mushrooms with a paper towel and inspect them for more dirt to wipe or rinse off.

GRILLED CORN WITH CILANTRO PESTO

Gluten-free, Vegan • Serves 6

This entire side dish is made on the grill, so cleanup is minimal. It is best made with fresh white corn, which we get in Maryland every summer. Serve it with the Steak with Everything Marinade (page 60) at a barbecue.

PREP TIME: 5 minutes • COOK TIME: 28 minutes • ADVANCE PREP: May be made 2 days in advance • EQUIPMENT: Measuring cups and spoons, cutting board, knife, food processor, silicone spatula, tongs, plastic wrap, plate or pan, large bowl

3 cloves garlic

2 cups (80g) packed cilantro leaves, including some stems

2 tablespoons plus 1 teaspoon sunflower or safflower oil

1 teaspoon tamari soy sauce

1 teaspoon sesame oil

⅛ teaspoon black pepper

Salt to taste

1 red bell pepper, halved and seeds removed

4 scallions, ends trimmed

8 ears of fresh corn, husked

Kosher salt (optional)

• Preheat the grill to medium-high, so the heat stays at 550°F (290°C).

• Place the garlic in the bowl of a food processor and process until finely ground. Add the cilantro leaves and process until the leaves are in very tiny pieces. Scrape down the bowl and process again for a few more seconds. Add 2 tablespoons of the sunflower oil, soy sauce, sesame oil, black pepper, and a little salt, and process until it is all mixed together.

Place all of the vegetables on the grill as follows:

• Rub the remaining 1 teaspoon of oil on the red pepper halves and place them, skin side down, on the grill. Cook the peppers until they're blackened, about 10 to 12 minutes. When they're black, transfer them to a bowl, cover it with plastic, and let the peppers sit for at least 15 minutes.

• Place the scallions on the grill and cook them until they're charred, but not falling apart, about 4 to 5 minutes. Watch carefully.

• Shmear half the pesto all over the ears of corn and cook them for 10 to 12 minutes, turning them every 3 to 4 minutes, until they're charred on all sides. Transfer the corn to a plate or pan and let them cool until you can handle them.

• Peel off the charred skin of the red pepper and discard. Cut pepper into ½-inch (12-mm) pieces. Place them in a large serving bowl. Cut the kernels off the cobs and add the kernels to the bowl. Slice the scallions into ½-inch (12-mm) pieces. Add the remaining pesto to the bowl and mix well. Taste the mixture and add a little kosher salt and black pepper, if needed.

SRI LANKAN RICE WITH DRIED FRUITS AND NUTS

Gluten-free, Vegan • Serves 4 to 6

Imagine my surprise when I learned two ways to make rice more digestible, more nutritious, and less caloric. First I discovered that soaking rice in water and an acid for at least seven hours or overnight neutralizes the phytic acid that prevents the absorption of key minerals, and soaking breaks down certain proteins, making the rice more digestible. Then researchers in Sri Lanka developed a method of adding coconut oil to the rice, cooking it as you normally would, and then chilling it for 12 hours before reheating and eating it, thereby reducing the calories in the rice by 10 percent. Clearly, these methods require planning but not much added work. The addition of herbs, spices, nuts, and fruit is my nod to those wonderful rice mixes you can buy at Machane Yehuda Market in Jerusalem. This recipe has an estimated amount of dried fruit that, when chopped, adds up to 1 cup. You can mix and match the ones you like best. You can make this recipe with 1 cup of any kind of rice (3 cups cooked) and omit the soaking and chilling if you are pressed for time.

PREP TIME: Soak rice for 7 hours (optional); chill cooked rice for 12 hours (optional) • COOK TIME: Rice: 15 minutes; assembly: 15 minutes • ADVANCE PREP: May be made 3 days in advance • EQUIPMENT: Measuring cups and spoons, citrus juicer, cutting board, knife, small saucepan with lid, silicone spatula, fork, large saucepan, small bowl, large frying pan

1 cup (160g) white rice (basmati or jasmine)

2 cups (480ml) water

2 tablespoons lemon juice or apple cider vinegar

2 teaspoons coconut oil

¾ teaspoon ground turmeric, divided

½ cup (60g) slivered almonds

2 tablespoons extra virgin olive oil

1 large onion, chopped into ½-inch (12-mm) pieces

5 pitted dates, chopped into ½-inch (12-mm) pieces

5 dried apricots, chopped into ½-inch (12-mm) pieces

3 dried figs

4 prunes, chopped into ½-inch (12-mm) pieces

½ teaspoon ground cumin

¼ teaspoon paprika

¼ teaspoon ground cinnamon

¼ teaspoon kosher salt

¼ teaspoon black pepper

2 tablespoons chopped fresh dill

2 tablespoons chopped fresh parsley

• Place the rice, water, and lemon juice in a small saucepan. Stir and cover the rice, and let it sit for at least 7 hours.

• Add the coconut oil and ½ teaspoon of the turmeric to the saucepan and then bring the rice to a boil. Cover and cook the rice for a little less time than the directions on the package, or until the water is absorbed. Let the rice cool, fluff it with a fork to separate the grains, and then refrigerate it for 12 hours or overnight.

• Heat a large saucepan over medium heat. Add the almonds and cook them, stirring them often, until they are toasted and golden. Transfer the almonds to a small bowl to let them cool. Add the olive oil to the pan and add the onions. Cook the onions for 5 minutes, or until they are lightly browned.

• Add the dates, apricots, figs, prunes, cumin, remaining ¼ teaspoon turmeric, paprika, and cinnamon and mix well. Cook the mixture for 2 minutes. Add the rice and cook it for 5 minutes, stirring it often and breaking up any clumps of rice. Add the salt and pepper, then taste to see if you need more. Add herbs and mix them in well.

• Place the rice in a serving bowl and sprinkle the almonds on top.

As a French-trained pastry chef, I prioritize taste when developing dessert recipes. When I host Shabbat and holiday meals, my next priority is ease of preparation. This chapter challenged me beyond those priorities—to create delicious dessert recipes that are also better for my family's health. It wasn't easy. I started with my favorite Jewish recipes and reworked them to include more whole grains, remove all gluten where possible, and reduce the large amounts of sugar, salt, and fat that are typical of Jewish dessert recipes in many cookbooks.

I swore off margarine, commercial puff pastry, and non-dairy creamers, and I developed a relationship with coconut oil as well as whole-grain flours. I tried to use less than a cup (200g) of sugar in each dessert recipe, and if you find 1 cup in a recipe or two, rest assured that I tried reducing that amount, but could not do so without compromising taste. I worked hard to select ingredients that are easy to find. Ultimately, I am proud of this chapter and will prove to you that you can enjoy delicious desserts that are better for you. I will still tell you, though, that portion size matters, and that you need to exercise if you want to eat baked goods regularly. My goal is to move your thinking, baking, and taste buds in a new, healthier direction.

Desserts *and* Breads

MATCHA MANDEL BREAD WITH ALMONDS, PISTACHIOS, AND CRANBERRIES

Parve • Makes about 60 thin cookies

I discovered desserts made with matcha green tea powder when I traveled to Japan and Hong Kong several years ago. There is a recipe for green tea hamantaschen in *The Holiday Kosher Baker* (Sterling, 2013) that is still one of my favorite recipes and demonstrates how much I like to mix up culinary traditions in the recipes I develop. Green tea contains antioxidants, and you can buy the powder in health food stores or online.

PREP TIME: 10 minutes; cookies need to cool 1½ hours before slicing • BAKE TIME: 15 minutes to toast almonds; 38 minutes to bake cookies • ADVANCE PREP: May be made 4 days in advance or frozen • EQUIPMENT: Measuring cups and spoons, citrus juicer, Microplane zester, cutting board, knife, small bowl, mixing bowl, electric mixer with whisk attachment or wooden spoon, 2 jelly roll pans or cookie sheets, parchment paper or silicone baking mats, silicone spatula

1 cup (150g) whole almonds, with or without skin

2½ cups (190g) all-purpose flour

½ cup (65g) whole-wheat flour

1 cup (200g) sugar

2 teaspoons baking powder

2 teaspoons matcha/green tea powder

¼ teaspoon salt

¼ cup (60ml) orange juice (from 1 orange)

3 large eggs

½ cup (120g) sunflower, safflower or canola oil

1 teaspoon lemon zest (from 1 lemon)

1 cup (140g) dried cranberries, roughly chopped

¾ cup (90g) shelled pistachios

• Preheat oven to 325°F (160°C). Place the whole almonds onto a jelly roll pan or large cookie sheet and bake them for 12 to 15 minutes, or until they're fragrant. Stir the nuts or shake the pan after 10 minutes. Transfer the nuts to a bowl and let them cool for 10 minutes, while you make the dough.

• Raise oven heat to 350°F (180°C). Line one of the pans with parchment paper or a silicone baking mat.

• In a large bowl, mix together the all-purpose flour, whole-wheat flour, sugar, baking powder, matcha green tea powder, salt, orange juice, eggs, oil, and lemon zest, until the dough comes together. Add the whole toasted almonds, cranberries, and pistachios and mix them in.

• Divide the dough in half and shape each half into a log, about 10 to 12 inches (25 to 30cm) long by 3 to 5 inches (7.5 to 12cm) wide. Place the 2 loaves on the prepared pan, about 5 inches (12cm) apart. Flatten each loaf slightly.

• Bake the loaves for 25 to 30 minutes, or until they look golden on top and a little browned on the bottom. Slide the parchment or silicone baking mat off the pan. Let the loaves cool completely, for about 1½ hours.

• Move the loaves to a cutting board and slice each loaf crosswise into ⅓-inch-thick (8-mm) slices (thinner than you typically would for mandel bread) to make the cookies. Place a new piece of parchment on the pan and cover a second pan with another piece of parchment. Divide the cookies between the 2 pans and place the sliced cookies on the pans cut-side down. Place the pan in the oven and bake the cookies for 8 more minutes. Slide the parchment off the cookie sheet onto a cooling rack and let the cookies cool.

Cookie Sheets

For baking sweets and breads, always line your cookie sheets with parchment or a silicone baking mat.

Even if you set your oven to the "convection" setting, you should still rotate the cookie sheets (switch racks) halfway through baking.

Avoid disposable sheet pans that are flimsy, because cookies do not bake evenly on them. It is worth buying at least two good cookie sheets and then baking in batches. Heavy-gauge, light-colored aluminum pans are best, as darker-colored cookie sheets absorb too much heat and have a tendency to burn cookies.

BLUEBERRY HONEY CAKE SCONES

Dairy • Makes 11 to 12 scones

These scones taste like classic honey cake and are a great snack for Shabbat or a holiday afternoon. I like to reheat them on the second or third day. You can make them parve, but they are much better baked with butter.

PREP TIME: 10 minutes • BAKE TIME: 13 to 17 minutes • ADVANCE PREP: May be made 3 days in advance or frozen • EQUIPMENT: Measuring cups and spoons, jelly roll pan or cookie sheet, parchment or silicone baking mats, spoon, food processor, knife, small bowl, fork, pastry brush, silicone spatula,

⅓ cup (75ml) strong hot coffee (prepared, not the grains; I use decaf espresso)

2 tablespoons honey, plus 1 teaspoon for glaze

2 tablespoons milk

1 cup (110ml) spelt flour

1 cup (125ml) all-purpose flour, plus 1 to 2 tablespoons extra for sprinkling and shaping

¼ cup (50g) sugar

1 tablespoon baking powder

1 teaspoon ground cinnamon

¾ teaspoon ground ginger

¼ teaspoon cloves

½ teaspoon ground nutmeg

6 tablespoons (84g) unsalted butter

2 large eggs, divided

1 cup (145g) blueberries

Eggs

Desserts come out best when eggs are at room temperature—the temperature of eggs affects the height and texture of baked goods. Use *large* eggs only as all baking recipes, unless otherwise stated, are calibrated with large eggs. Using extra large or jumbo eggs will make a recipe wetter and affect the result in unintended ways.

• Preheat the oven to 400°F (200°C). Cover a cookie sheet or jelly roll pan with parchment paper or a silicone baking mat.

• Measure the hot coffee into a liquid measuring cup and add the 2 tablespoons of honey. Stir the mixture to dissolve the honey and let it cool for 10 minutes. Add the milk and stir.

• Place the spelt flour and all-purpose flour in the bowl of a food processor. Add the sugar, baking powder, cinnamon, ginger, cloves, and nutmeg and process for 10 seconds.

• Cut the butter into six pieces and add them to the bowl. Process for 10 seconds.

• Using a fork, beat an egg in a small bowl and add it to the food processor bowl. Add the coffee mixture and process just until the dough comes together. Be careful not to overmix.

• Sprinkle 1 tablespoon of all-purpose flour on the counter or parchment paper. Transfer the dough from the food processor bowl onto the floured surface. Knead the dough by folding it over a few times and mixing in the flour, until it is soft.

• Flatten the dough into a circle and then press in a handful of blueberries. Fold the dough in half over the blueberries and then press in another handful of berries. (Flour your hands if the dough starts to stick to them.) Keep folding the dough over the berries and adding the blueberries until they are all mixed in and well distributed.

• Cut the dough in half. Use your hands to roll each piece into a 2-inch-thick (5-cm) log, about 7 inches (17cm) long. Using a sharp knife with a flat edge, cut the dough into triangles, first cutting on an angle to the right, and then cutting on an angle to the left. Try to make the triangles about the same size. You will have about 5 triangles per log, with a little dough leftover. Place the triangles on the prepared cookie sheet. Repeat the process with the second log and then press together any remaining smaller pieces of the dough and shape it into a rectangle the size of the other triangles. Beat the remaining egg into the cup you used for the coffee, add the remaining teaspoon honey and stir, and then brush the top of the scones with the egg wash.

• Bake the scones for 13 to 17 minutes, or until the tops are just beginning to brown. Let the scones cool for 5 minutes. Serve them warm or at room temperature.

PUMPKIN HAMANTASCHEN

Parve • Makes 3 dozen cookies

Purim is one of my favorite Jewish holidays, and I love to invent new flavors of hamantaschen every year. These taste best when they are baked until firm.

PREP TIME: 10 minutes; 1 hour to chill dough; 15 minutes to roll out and shape • BAKE TIME: 14 minutes • ADVANCE PREP: May be made 2 days in advance; avoid freezing • EQUIPMENT: Measuring cups and spoons, can opener, large bowl, electric mixer, silicone spatula, plastic wrap, medium bowl, 2 jelly roll pans or cookie sheets, parchment paper or silicone baking mats, rolling pin, small drinking glass or round cookie cutter (2 to 3 inches [5 to 7.5cm] in diameter), long metal flat-blade spatula

DOUGH

3 large eggs

1 cup (200g) sugar

½ cup (120g) sunflower, safflower, or canola oil

½ cup (113g) pumpkin purée

1 teaspoon pure vanilla extract

½ teaspoon ground cinnamon

¼ teaspoon ground nutmeg

1¾ cups (220g) all-purpose flour, plus extra for dusting

1¼ cups (163g) whole-wheat flour

Dash salt

FILLING

1 cup (225g) pumpkin purée

¼ cup (55g) light brown sugar

½ teaspoon ground cinnamon

1 teaspoon maple syrup

1 large egg yolk

• In a large bowl, use an electric mixer to mix together the eggs, sugar, oil, pumpkin purée, and vanilla and mix well. Add the cinnamon, nutmeg, all-purpose flour, whole-wheat flour, and salt and mix until the dough comes together. Form the dough into a round,

then cover it with plastic wrap and place it in the fridge for 1 hour or overnight to firm up.

• Prepare the filling. In a medium bowl, place the pumpkin purée, light brown sugar, cinnamon, maple syrup, and egg yolk and mix well. Cover and refrigerate until you are ready to roll out the dough.

• Preheat the oven to 375°F (190°C). Line 2 to 3 cookie sheets or jelly roll pans with parchment or silicone baking mats. Divide the dough in half.

• Cut off 2 pieces of parchment paper and sprinkle all-purpose flour on one. Place a dough half on top of the parchment paper, then sprinkle flour on top of the dough. Place the second piece of parchment on top of the dough and, using a rolling pin, roll over the top of the parchment paper. Roll out the dough until it is about ¼-inch (6-mm) thick. After every few rolls, peel back the top parchment and sprinkle a little more flour on the dough. Once or twice, flip over the parchment-dough "package" and peel off the bottom parchment. Sprinkle a little flour on top of the dough, place the parchment back on top, and then flip it over.

• Lift off the top parchment. Using a small drinking glass or a round cookie cutter, cut the dough into circles. Using a long metal flat-blade spatula to lift the cookie circles and place them on a piece of parchment paper sprinkled with a little flour. Place ¾ to 1 teaspoon of filling in the center of each dough circle, and then fold in the three sides toward the middle to form a triangle, leaving a small opening in the center. Pinch the three sides together very tightly. Place the cookies on the prepared baking sheets. Repeat the process with the remaining dough. Roll and cut any extra dough scraps, making sure to sprinkle a little flour under and over the dough before you roll it out.

• Bake the cookies for 14 minutes, or until they are lightly browned. These cookies taste best when they are crunchy. Slide the parchment and cookies onto wire cooling racks.

ISRAELI CHOCOLATE RUGELACH

Parve or Dairy (depending on yogurt and milk) • Makes 48 cookies

These rugelach are inspired by the popular Marzipan Bakery rugelach that are sold in the Machane Yehuda Market in Jerusalem. Mine are made with more than 50 percent whole-grain flour. I use dairy-free coconut yogurt in the dough, but you can also use dairy yogurt, or soy sour cream instead. The rugelach in Israel are covered with a thick sugary glaze, so I have created an optional honey glaze to brush on top.

PREP TIME: 8 minutes for dough; dough rises for 1 to 1½ hours; 15 minutes to shape the rugelach • BAKE TIME: 12 to 13 minutes • ADVANCE PREP: May be made 3 days in advance or frozen • EQUIPMENT: Measuring cups and spoons, stand mixer, plastic wrap, large microwave-safe bowl, large silicone spatula, 2 to 3 cookie sheets or jelly roll pans, parchment or silicone baking mats, large flat-blade knife or pizza cutter, rolling pin, small microwave-safe bowl or small saucepan, pastry brush

DOUGH

2 envelopes (½ ounce [15g]) active dry yeast

½ cup (120ml) warm water

2 tablespoons plus 1 teaspoon sugar, divided

⅓ cup (80ml) regular yogurt, dairy-free coconut yogurt, or soy sour cream

2 large egg yolks

8 tablespoons unsalted coconut oil (120ml) or butter (112g; at room temperature)

1¼ cups (163g) whole-wheat flour

1 cup (125g) all-purpose flour, plus more for sprinkling

2 teaspoons pure vanilla extract

¼ teaspoon salt

FILLING

10 ounces (280g) bittersweet chocolate, broken into pieces

⅓ cup (80ml) any type of milk (soy or almond if making dairy-free)

2 tablespoons dark, unsweetened cocoa

2 tablespoons vanilla sugar or regular sugar plus 1 teaspoon pure vanilla extract

HONEY GLAZE

2 tablespoons honey

2 teaspoons water

• In the bowl of a stand mixer, place the yeast, warm water, and 1 teaspoon sugar, stir, and let the mixture sit for 8 to 10 minutes or until it has become thick. Add the yogurt, egg yolks, coconut oil, whole-wheat flour, all-purpose-flour, vanilla, and salt, and mix with the hook attachment until it comes together to form a smooth dough. Cover the bowl with plastic wrap and let the dough rise for 1 to 1½ hours at room temperature.

• Ten minutes before rolling out the dough, prepare the filling. Place the chocolate in a large microwave-safe bowl. Heat the chocolate for 1 minute and stir; heat it for 45 seconds and stir again; heat the chocolate for 30 seconds or longer, until it has melted. Add the milk, cocoa, and vanilla sugar, and combine well. Let the mixture sit for 5 minutes.

• Preheat the oven to 350°F (180°C). Line 3 cookie sheets or jelly roll pans with parchment paper, or bake them in batches if you have only one or two baking sheets. Divide the dough into 3 pieces.

• To roll out each piece of dough, place a large piece of parchment paper on the counter and sprinkle all-purpose flour on top. Add the dough and sprinkle more flour on top. Roll the dough into a 9 x 14-inch (23 x 36-cm) rectangle. Try your best to roll it into a rectangle. You will need to sprinkle more flour on the dough each time it sticks to the rolling pin, and lift up the dough a few times to sprinkle some flour underneath it to make sure it does not stick to the parchment paper.

• Use a large silicone spatula to scoop up a third of the filling and spread to the edges of the dough. Using a pizza cutter or knife, slice across the dough the long way to create two long rectangles. Slice the rectangles the other way into 4 equal rectangles, and then slice each of them in half to create 8 rectangles. Slice each rectangle in half from corner to corner to make 16 long triangles.

• Roll up each triangle from the shorter base to the point and then bend in the corners to create a crescent shape. Place the cookies on the prepared baking sheet, leaving a little space between each cookie. Bake them for 12 to 13 minutes, or until they are lightly browned. Repeat the process with the other 2 balls of dough. If the filling gets too thick to spread, heat it in the microwave for a few minutes.

• While the rugelach are baking, prepare the honey syrup. Place the honey and water in a bowl and put it in a microwave oven for 15 seconds, or until it's hot and the honey has dissolved. Alternatively, you can heat the water and dissolve the honey in a small saucepan on the stovetop. Mix well.

• Remove the cookies from the oven. Use a pastry brush to apply the glaze to the tops of the cookies. Serve warm immediately or at room temperature.

Melting Chocolate

Break or chop the chocolate into 1-inch (2.5-cm) pieces. You can melt the chocolate in a double boiler—or fashion your own from a bowl that sits atop a medium saucepan. Simply put about 2 inches (5cm) of water into the saucepan, place a glass or metal dish on top, making sure the dish doesn't touch the water, then put the chopped chocolate into the dish. Bring the water to a simmer; the steam will gently melt the chocolate in the bowl. Stir the chocolate occasionally until it melts.

Vanilla Sugar

If you cannot find vanilla sugar in the store, you can make your own: Just split a whole vanilla bean in half lengthwise, scrape the seeds out with a knife, and then place both the seeds and bean halves inside a jar with 2 cups (400g) of sugar. Or you can mix 1 teaspoon of vanilla extract into 2 cups (400g) of regular sugar.

GRANOLA BARS

Parve, Vegan, Gluten-free (if using gluten-free oats) • Makes 16 to 24 bars, depending on cut

While I was testing this recipe for granola bars, my son Sam was hiking the Pacific Crest Trail. I sent one of the first batches to Lone Pine, California, where Sam was resting and restocking his supplies for the next leg of the hike. Even though the granola bars weren't perfect yet, Sam loved getting a bite from home. Clearly, these bars can be shipped across the country and still taste great. When you slice these, smaller pieces of granola bars will remain on your cutting board; place these pieces into a baggie and save to eat with yogurt for breakfast or snack.

PREP TIME: 10 minutes; bars chill for 30 minutes before slicing • BAKE TIME: 50 minutes • ADVANCE PREP: May be made 5 days in advance or frozen • EQUIPMENT: Measuring cups and spoons, Microplane zester, cutting board, knife, 9 x 13-inch (23 x 33-cm) pan, large bowl, parchment, small saucepan, silicone spatula wooden spoon, large silicone spatula

2 cups oats, regular or gluten-free (not Irish or quick-cooking oats)

1½ cups (180g) slivered almonds

¾ cup (90g) pecan halves

¼ cup (40g) roasted peanuts

Cooking spray

⅓ cup (80ml) honey

2 tablespoons maple syrup

2 tablespoons brown sugar

½ teaspoon orange zest (from 1 orange)

¼ cup (40g) flaxseeds

¼ cup (35g) sunflower seeds

1 cup (145g) dried cherries, chopped roughly

½ cup (70g) dried cranberries

1 cup (125g) dates, pitted and chopped into ½-inch (12-mm) pieces

¼ teaspoon ground ginger

½ teaspoon ground cinnamon

⅓ cup (80g) unsweetened applesauce

• Preheat the oven to 350°F (180°C). Place the oats, almonds, pecans, and peanuts in a 9 x 13-inch (23 x 33-cm) pan and toss them together. Toast the mix for 20 minutes, or until the almonds start to brown. Remove the mixture from the oven and place it in a large bowl. Let it cool for 10 minutes. Reduce the oven temperature to 325°F (160°C). Prepare the pan with cooking spray and line it with parchment paper, making sure that it goes up the sides of the pan. Spray the top of the parchment paper.

• Place the honey, maple syrup, brown sugar, and orange zest into a small saucepan. Bring the mixture to a boil over medium heat, stir it, and then let it simmer on low heat for 5 minutes.

• When the nut mixture has cooled, add the flaxseeds, sunflower seeds, dried cherries, chopped dates, ginger, and cinnamon and mix well. Break apart any clumps that form around the dates. Pour the honey mixture over the nut mixture and stir well. Add the applesauce and mix. Scoop the mixture into the prepared pan and use a large silicone spatula or your hands to press the mixture down as tightly as possible.

• Bake the mixture for 30 minutes. Let it cool for 30 minutes, and then freeze it for 30 minutes. Slice it into rectangular bars and store at room temperature for up to 7 days—or until the bars are gone.

CHOCOLATE QUINOA CAKE

Parve, Gluten-free, Passover (without pure vanilla extract) • Serves 12

I had heard the myth of chocolate cakes made with cooked quinoa and didn't quite believe they'd actually be tasty. This cake is surprisingly moist and delicious—great for Passover and all year round.

PREP TIME: 20 minutes • BAKE TIME: 15 minutes to cook quinoa, 50 minutes to bake cake • ADVANCE PREP: May be made 3 days in advance or frozen • EQUIPMENT: Measuring cups and spoons, small saucepan with lid, 12-cup (2.8L) Bundt pan, food processor, medium microwave-safe bowl or double boiler, silicone spatula, wooden kebab skewer, wire cooling rack, large microwave-safe bowl, whisk

CAKE

¾ cup (130g) quinoa

1½ cups (360ml) water

Cooking spray

2 tablespoons potato starch

⅓ cup (80ml) orange juice (from 1 orange)

4 large eggs

2 teaspoons pure vanilla extract (or other vanilla if for Passover)

¾ cup (180ml) coconut oil

1½ cups (300g) sugar

1 cup (80g) dark unsweetened cocoa

2 teaspoons baking powder

½ teaspoon salt

2 ounces (55g) bittersweet chocolate

Fresh raspberries, for garnish (optional)

GLAZE (OPTIONAL)

5 ounces (140g) bittersweet chocolate

1 tablespoon sunflower or safflower oil

1 teaspoon pure vanilla extract (or other vanilla if for Passover)

• Place the quinoa and water into a small saucepan and bring it to a boil over medium heat. Reduce the heat to low, cover the saucepan, and cook the quinoa for 15 minutes, or until all the liquid has been absorbed. Set the pan aside. The quinoa may be made 1 day in advance.

• Preheat the oven to 350°F (180°C). Use cooking spray to grease a 12-cup (2.8L) Bundt pan. Sprinkle the potato starch over the greased pan and then shake the pan to remove any excess starch.

• Place the quinoa in the bowl of a food processor. Add the orange juice, eggs, vanilla, oil, sugar, cocoa, baking powder, and salt and process until the mixture is very smooth.

• Melt the chocolate over a double boiler, or place in a medium microwave-safe bowl, and put in a microwave for 45 seconds, stirring and then heating the chocolate for another 30 seconds, until it is melted. Add the chocolate to the quinoa batter and process until well mixed. Pour the batter into the prepared Bundt pan and bake it for 50 minutes, or until a skewer inserted into the cake comes out clean.

• Let the cake cool for 10 minutes and then remove it gently from the pan. Let it cool on a wire cooling rack.

• To make the glaze, melt the chocolate in a large microwave-safe bowl in the microwave (see above) or over a double boiler. Add the oil and vanilla and whisk well. Let the glaze sit for 5 minutes and then whisk it again. Use a silicone spatula to spread the glaze all over the cake.

ROOT VEGETABLE AND APPLE CAKE

Parve • Serves 12 to 16

No Jewish New Year is complete without an apple cake, so here is one you can feel good about, as it contains two kinds of vegetables.

PREP TIME: 8 minutes • BAKE TIME: 45 minutes • ADVANCE PREP: May be made 2 days in advance • EQUIPMENT: Vegetable peeler, cutting board, knife, measuring cups and spoons, citrus juicer, box grater, shallow bowl, large mixing bowl, 8-inch (20-cm) square baking pan, silicone spatula or wooden spoon, wooden kebab skewer

Cooking spray

1 large or 2 small Gala apples, peeled, cored, and cut into ¼-inch wedges

1 tablespoon light brown sugar

3 large eggs

½ cup (120ml) sunflower or safflower oil

⅓ cup (65g) sugar

½ cup (75g) brown sugar

⅓ cup (80ml) orange juice (from 2½ oranges)

2 teaspoons pure vanilla extract

½ cup (65g) all-purpose flour

½ cup (65g) whole-wheat flour

½ teaspoon ground nutmeg

1 teaspoon ground ginger

1 teaspoon baking powder

¼ teaspoon salt

1 teaspoon ground cinnamon

½ cup (55g) grated carrots (from 1 peeled carrot, using the small holes of a box grater)

⅔ cup (85g) grated parsnips (from 1 peeled parsnip, using the small holes of a box grater)

• Preheat the oven to 350°F (180°C). Grease an 8-inch (20-cm) square baking pan with cooking spray.

• Place the apple wedges and brown sugar in a shallow bowl, and toss to coat. Transfer the apple wedges to the bottom of a pan in rows, in one layer, overlapping them if necessary. Use small pieces of apple to fill in any holes.

• Place the eggs, oil, sugar, brown sugar, orange juice, and vanilla in a large bowl, and mix well. Add the all-purpose flour, whole-wheat flour, nutmeg, ginger, baking powder, salt, and cinnamon to the bowl and mix well. Add the grated carrots and parsnips to the bowl and mix them into the batter. Pour the batter over the apples and spread it evenly.

• Bake the cake for 45 minutes, or until the top is browned and a wooden kebab skewer inserted into the cake comes out clean. Let it cool for 30 minutes and then turn it over onto a serving platter. Serve at room temperature.

Greasing pans

The best way to grease a cake pan is to use a baking spray, which contains flour. You can also grease the pan with regular cooking spray, add 2 tablespoons of flour or potato starch to the pan, shake it all around, and then tap out the excess flour. When I use round, square, or rectangular baking pans, I often trace the bottom of the pan on parchment paper, cut out the shape, grease the pan with oil, press in the cut parchment, and then grease the top of the parchment. This method makes it super easy to pop a cake out of the pan and makes it easier to clean.

Testing doneness

Toothpicks are too short to insert into a large cake to test for doneness. Instead, buy long wooden kebab skewers and store them near your oven; they allow you to test the deepest part of your cake. Once the inserted skewer comes out clean, the cake is done.

KHEER: INDIAN-SPICED RICE PUDDING

Parve, Gluten-free, Vegan • Serves 8

Rice pudding will always remind me of my grandma Sylvia, who made the classic dairy version. Here, I've replaced milk with thick coconut milk. You can use cardamom pods or ground cardamom, but the pods give the pudding more flavor.

PREP TIME: 5 minutes; 12 hours to chill • COOK TIME: 35 minutes • ADVANCE PREP: May be made 3 days in advance • EQUIPMENT: Can opener, measuring cups and spoons, cutting board, knife, 8-cup (2-quart) measuring cup, medium heavy saucepan, sieve or flour sifter, mortar and pestle or coffee grinder or spice grinder, whisk, silicone spatula

2 13.5-ounce (385-g) cans coconut milk (thick kind)

½ cup (90g) raw basmati rice, rinsed well

⅔ cup (130g) sugar

12 cardamom pods or ½ teaspoon ground cardamom

3 generous pinches saffron threads

¼ cup (30g) slivered almonds, roughly chopped

2 tablespoons golden raisins

⅓ cup (40g) cashews, roughly chopped

Sliced mango, for garnish

• Pour the coconut milk into an 8-cup (2-quart) measuring pitcher. Fill each can with water and pour it into the pitcher with the coconut milk. Add enough water to total 6 cups (1.4L). Pour the coconut milk and water mixture into a medium saucepan and bring it to a boil over medium-high heat.

• Add the rice and sugar to the saucepan and cook it uncovered over low heat for 20 minutes, whisking it a few times. While the pudding is cooking, grind the cardamom pods as finely as possible, using a mortar and pestle or a coffee grinder or spice grinder.

• Shake the ground cardamom through a fine sieve or flour sifter to separate the powder from pieces of the cardamom pod. Add just the powder to the pudding. Add the saffron threads and thoroughly mix them in. Add the almonds and golden raisins and whisk them into the pudding.

• Cook the pudding for another 10 minutes, stirring it occasionally. Add the cashews and let the pudding cool for 30 minutes. Transfer it to a serving bowl. Cover and chill the pudding in the fridge for at least 12 hours before serving. Serve with mango, if desired.

> ### Using a Coffee Grinder for Spices and Nuts
>
> I have a separate coffee grinder in my kitchen that I use to grind spices and nuts into a powder for use in sweet and savory recipes. If you use the same coffee grinder to grind coffee, spices, and nuts, make sure to wipe out the inside of the grinder bowl with a damp paper towel both before and after using it to grind the spices and nuts.

SPELT CHOCOLATE BABKA

Parve • Makes I loaf

My chocolate babka is the dessert I am best known for, but as I've traveled the world teaching people how to make it, this dessert has also elicited the most criticism, because of the amount of parve margarine in the original recipe. My defense has always focused on portion control: If you eat just one slice, then it won't be that bad for you. However, as a mother of twins who absolutely want their babka prepared the original way, I knew I was on to something when this recipe (which is made without any margarine!) won them over. Here's a babka you can feel good about.

PREP TIME: 13 minutes for dough; first rising 1 to 1½ hours; 10 minutes to prepare filling and assemble; second rising 30 minutes • BAKE TIME: 30 minutes • ADVANCE PREP: May be made 3 days in advance or frozen • EQUIPMENT: Measuring cups and spoons, stand mixer, plastic wrap, medium microwave-safe bowl, silicone spatula, whisk, 12-inch (30-cm) loaf pan, parchment, kitchen scissors, rolling pin, long flat-blade knife

DOUGH

¼ cup (60ml) water

2 envelopes (½ ounce [15g]) active dry yeast

⅓ cup (65g) plus 1 teaspoon sugar, divided

1½ cups (165g) spelt flour, plus extra for dusting

¾ cup (95g) all-purpose flour

½ cup (65g) whole-wheat flour

¼ cup (60ml) sunflower or other mild oil

6 tablespoons (90ml) coconut oil or spread

1 teaspoon pure vanilla extract

2 large eggs, plus 1 egg white
  (reserve 1 yolk for glaze)

FILLING

5 ounces (140g) bittersweet chocolate,
  broken into small squares

2 tablespoons sugar

¼ cup (20g) dark unsweetened cocoa

2 tablespoons sunflower or other mild oil

Cooking spray

¾ cup (125g) chocolate chips

• Place the water, yeast, and 1 teaspoon of the sugar in the bowl of a stand mixer. Mix and let sit for 8 to 10 minutes, or until thick. Add the remaining ⅓ cup (65g) sugar, spelt flour, all-purpose flour, whole-wheat flour, sunflower oil, coconut oil, vanilla, 2 eggs, and 1 egg white to the mixture. Combine it by hand or use a dough hook attachment until all the ingredients are mixed together. Cover the bowl with plastic wrap and let the dough rise for 1½ to 2 hours, or until it is spongy.

• When the dough is almost ready to be rolled out, place the bittersweet chocolate in a microwave-safe medium glass bowl. Heat the chocolate in the microwave oven for 1 minute and stir. Heat it for another 45 seconds and stir, and then heat for another 30 seconds, if needed, and stir until it is completely melted. Add the sugar, cocoa, and oil to the chocolate, and whisk it well. Place the mixture in the freezer for 5 minutes. Whisk it again.

• Use cooking spray to grease a 12-inch (30-cm) loaf pan. Trace the bottom of the loaf pan onto a piece of parchment paper and cut it out. Place the rectangle on the bottom of the pan and spray it.

• Place a large piece of parchment paper on your counter. Sprinkle a little spelt flour on top of it. Roll out the dough until it is about 12 x 18 inches (30 to 33cm) to 13 x 19 inches (46 to 48cm). Spread the filling over the dough, all the way to the edges. Sprinkle the chocolate chips over the top of the filling and roll up the dough the long way.

• Wrap the roll in the parchment paper and place in the freezer for 5 minutes to firm up. Remove the roll from the freezer, unwrap it with the seam on the bottom, and use a large flat-blade knife to slice it in half lengthwise. Turn each half of the roll so that the cut sides face up and drape over each other in an "X." On each side of the "X," twist the 2 strands over and under each other, keeping the cut side facing up. Tuck the ends under the loaf so that they touch or slightly overlap each other in the center.

• Place the loaf in the prepared pan.

• Let the babka rise for 30 minutes. Brush the top with the reserved egg yolk mixed with 1 teaspoon of water. Preheat the oven to 350°F (180°C). Bake the babka for 30 minutes, or until it is golden brown. Let it cool for 10 minutes and then turn it out onto a wire cooling rack.

CARAMELIZED APPLE STRUDEL

Parve, Vegan • Serves 10 to 12

Apple strudel is one of those Old World desserts that few people bake from scratch anymore. The whole-grain dough in this recipe is very easy to make and roll out. I like to rewarm the strudel after the first day.

PREP TIME: 20 minutes; dough rises 1 to 2 hours • BAKE TIME: 30 to 40 minutes • ADVANCE PREP: May be made 2 days in advance; reheat to serve • EQUIPMENT: Measuring cups and spoons, vegetable peeler, cutting board, knife, stand mixer without attachment, plastic wrap, large frying pan, wooden spoon, silicone spatula, cookie sheet or jelly roll pan, parchment or silicone baking mat, wire cooling rack

DOUGH

½ cup (65g) plus 2 tablespoons (15g) all-purpose flour, plus extra for dusting

½ cup (65g) white whole-wheat flour

½ cup (65g) whole-wheat flour

1 tablespoon sugar

¼ teaspoon salt

¼ cup (60ml) sunflower or safflower oil

½ cup (120ml) water

Honey to drizzle over the strudel (optional)

FILLING

2 tablespoons coconut oil

¼ cup (55g) light brown sugar

1 tablespoon sugar

½ teaspoon cinnamon

4 Gala apples, peeled, cored, and sliced into ½-inch (12-mm) slices

3 tablespoons ground almonds

• To make the dough, place the all-purpose flour, white whole-wheat flour, whole-wheat flour, sugar, salt, oil, and water into the bowl of a stand mixer and mix with a dough hook attachment, or by hand, until it comes together into a ball. Cover the bowl with plastic wrap and let it rest for 1 to 2 hours at room temperature.

• To prepare the filling, heat a large frying pan over medium heat and add the coconut oil, brown sugar, sugar, and cinnamon, and stir. Add the apples to the pan and cook them, stirring often, for about 6 to 8 minutes, until the apples are fork-tender. Place the mixture into a bowl and let it cool for 10 minutes. Add the ground almonds and mix well.

• When the dough is ready, preheat the oven to 375°F (190°C). Divide the dough into 3 pieces. Cut off a large piece of parchment paper and sprinkle it with some all-purpose flour. Roll out a piece of dough into a rectangle about 8 x 14 inches (20 x 36cm), lifting the dough a few times to add more flour underneath it. Place a third of the filling down the length of the dough, 2 inches from the edge. Fold in the right and left sides (the short sides) about 1 inch from the edge. Roll the long end of the dough (with the filling), into a tight, long log. Place it on a cookie sheet or jelly roll pan lined with parchment or a silicone baking mat. Repeat the same steps to make 2 other logs.

• Bake the strudel for 30 to 40 minutes, or until it is lightly browned, and transfer to a wire cooling rack. Serve warm or at room temperature with a drizzle of honey over the top, if desired.

FRUIT COBBLER WITH CHICKPEA AND ALMOND TOPPING

Parve, Gluten-free • Serves 20

You can make this dessert with any combination of fruit, although my favorites are peaches, plums, and blueberries.

PREP TIME: 10 minutes • BAKE TIME: 40 minutes • ADVANCE PREP: May be made 3 days in advance and stored at room temperature for the first day; refrigerate thereafter • EQUIPMENT: Cutting board, knife, measuring cups and spoons, 9 x 13-inch (23 x 33-cm) pan, silicone spatula, food processor

FRUIT COBBLER

8 cups of fruit, cut into ¾-inch (2-cm) cubes (about 8 plums and 4 peaches, or 5 large apples), or you can use blueberries, raspberries, or blackberries, so long as the total amount of fruit is 8 cups

2 tablespoons honey

¼ cup (40g) potato starch, brown rice flour, or whole-wheat flour

TOPPING

2 cups (240g) slivered almonds

½ cup (120ml) coconut oil or spread

½ cup (55g) chickpea flour

½ cup (50g) ground almonds

⅓ cup (30g) oats (not quick cooking kind)

⅔ cup (150g) light brown sugar

1 tablespoon sugar

3 large eggs

2 teaspoons pure vanilla extract

¼ teaspoon ground cinnamon

¼ teaspoon baking powder

⅛ teaspoon salt

• Preheat the oven to 375°F (190°C). Place the prepared fruit into a 9 x 13-inch (23 x 33-cm) pan. Add the honey and potato starch to the pan, and toss the mixture until the starch dissolves.

• Place the almonds in the bowl of a food processor and chop them into small pieces. Add the coconut oil or spread, chickpea flour, ground almonds, oats, brown sugar, sugar, eggs, vanilla, cinnamon, baking powder, and salt and process until the mixture comes together. Spread it over the fruit, covering it as much as possible.

• Bake the cobbler for 40 minutes, or until the crumb topping is browned and the fruit starts to bubble. Let it cool for 10 minutes. Serve the cobbler warm. Reheat it to serve it again later.

Using Coconut Oil

Coconut oil and coconut spreads are the newest best friends of the dairy-free baker. The only problem is that many people simply do not like the taste of coconut. I have found that when I want to use coconut fat to replace margarine in a dessert, I simply add more vanilla, cinnamon, lemon, chocolate, or whatever flavor dominates the dessert, to mask the flavor of the coconut fat. Yes, you're tricking them, but it's for their benefit.

AQUAFABA CHOCOLATE MOUSSE

Parve, Gluten-free, Vegan • Serves 6

Aquafaba is the thick liquid in canned chickpeas that we usually dump down the drain of the kitchen sink. When I first heard that it's possible to make mousse out of this liquid, I didn't believe it until I tried it myself. When you beat chickpea liquid, it looks exactly like beaten egg whites, only they're vegan. Aquafaba really is magic—and tasty, too. After you've used the liquid from the can, you can use the chickpeas in the Chopped Salad with Lemon Sumac Dressing on page 4.

PREP TIME: 20 minutes; 12 hours to chill • **ADVANCE PREP:** May be made 3 days in advance • **EQUIPMENT:** Can opener, measuring cups and spoons, stand mixer with whisk attachment, large microwave-safe bowl, silicone spatula

Liquid from 1 15-ounce (430g) can chickpeas (reserve chickpeas for other use)

¼ teaspoon cream of tartar

3 tablespoons sugar

6 ounces (170g) bittersweet chocolate

• Place the chickpea liquid and cream of tartar into the bowl of a stand mixer fitted with the whisk attachment. Turn on the mixer to low speed for 1 minute, then turn it up to high and beat the chickpea liquid and tartar mixture with the whisk attachment for a full 15 minutes. Turn the speed to low and add the sugar, a little at a time, to the bowl. When the mixture is thoroughly mixed, turn the machine back to high and continue to beat for 1 minute or until thick and shiny.

• While the chickpea liquid is beating, place the chocolate in a microwave-safe bowl and heat it for 1 minute. Stir and heat the chocolate for 45 seconds, and then stir it again. Heat the chocolate for 30 seconds, or more, until it has completely melted. You can also melt the chocolate over a double boiler. Set it aside.

• Scoop up ¼ of the beaten chickpea liquid and sugar and whisk it into the melted chocolate. Add another ¼ of the beaten chickpea mix and whisk it in more slowly. Transfer this mixture to the bowl with the remaining beaten chickpea liquid and mix it in gently but thoroughly, so you don't see any white spots.

• Spoon the mousse into a large serving bowl or 6 individual bowls, cover them with plastic wrap, and let the mousse firm up for at least 12 hours.

MINI CHEESECAKES WITH OAT AND BROWN SUGAR CRUST AND STRAWBERRY PURÉE

Dairy, Gluten-free (if using gluten-free oats) • Serves 12

I truly love cheesecake, especially New York style, made only with cream cheese. These minis are lower in sugar than most cheesecakes, and they are gluten-free if you use gluten-free oat flour for the crust. Ricotta cheese pumps up the calcium content. I tried to make this recipe with lower fat cream cheese and ricotta, but the results were not satisfactory. The idea behind the mini cheesecakes was portion control, but I found myself grabbing them all day long, so I had to take extreme measures and freeze most of them to get them out of easy reach. I particularly like the buttery oat crust, which you could also use as a pie crust.

PREP TIME: 8 minutes; 4 hours to chill, 3 minutes for strawberry sauce • BAKE TIME: 10 minutes to bake crust, 25 minutes for cheesecake • ADVANCE PREP: May be made 3 days in advance or frozen (crust not as crunchy after freezing) • EQUIPMENT: Measuring cups and spoons, Microplane zester, cutting board, knife, 12-cup (2.8L) muffin pan and paper liners, medium microwave-safe bowl, silicone spatula, large bowl, electric mixer, food processor

CRUST

4 tablespoons (56g) unsalted butter

3 tablespoons (40g) light brown sugar

1 cup gluten-free oats (90g) (not quick-cooking kind)

2 tablespoons (12g) gluten-free oat flour or other flour

¼ teaspoon salt

CHEESECAKE

1 8-ounce (225-g) package cream cheese, at room temperature

3 large eggs

⅓ cup (65g) sugar

1 tablespoon gluten-free oat flour or other flour

2 teaspoons lemon zest (from 1 lemon)

1 teaspoon pure vanilla extract

1 cup (245g) whole milk ricotta cheese

Fresh strawberries, or other berries for garnish (optional)

STRAWBERRY PURÉE

2 cups (290g) trimmed fresh strawberries

1 tablespoon confectioners' sugar

• Preheat the oven to 350°F (180°C). To make the crust, place paper liners in a 12-cup (2.8L) muffin pan. Place the butter in a medium microwave-safe bowl and microwave for 1 minute, or until the butter melts. Add the brown sugar and mix well. Add the oats, oat flour, and salt and mix well. Place a heaping tablespoon of the mixture into each of the liners in the muffin pan and press it down. Use all of the oat mixture. Bake the crusts for 10 minutes, or until the edges start to color.

• Meanwhile, to make the filling, place the cream cheese in a large bowl. Beat it with an electric mixer on high speed until it is very smooth, scraping down the bowl a few times. Add the eggs into the cream cheese,

1 at a time, and beat them in. Scrape down the sides of the bowl. Add the sugar, oat flour, lemon zest, and vanilla to the bowl and mix for 1 minute. Add the ricotta and mix it in gently on low speed. Scoop about ⅓ cup (68g) of the mixture into each muffin cup.

• Bake the cheesecakes for 25 minutes, or until they've set. Let them cool in the pan and then refrigerate the cheesecakes for at least 4 hours.

• To make the strawberry purée, place the strawberries and confectioners' sugar in the bowl of a food processor and process until puréed. (Add water, a teaspoon at a time, if the strawberries are not very ripe and the mixture seems too dry.)

• Serve the mini cheesecakes with a spoonful of Strawberry Purée on top or on the side. Garnish with sliced fresh strawberries, or other berries, if desired.

FRUIT GALETTE WITH A CHOCOLATE CRUST

Parve • Serves 8

This galette is a new version of my easiest fruit tart. You do not even need a tart pan or pie plate. You can use any fruit you like, but it tastes best with summer fruits and it looks best if you combine raspberries and plums with peaches or apricots to contrast with the dark color of the chocolate crust.

PREP TIME: 5 minutes to make dough; 15 to 20 minutes for dough to chill; 10 minutes to fill and assemble tart • BAKE TIME: 30 minutes • ADVANCE PREP: May be made 2 days in advance • EQUIPMENT: Measuring cups and spoons, food processor or pastry cutter, cutting board, knife, plastic wrap, parchment or silicone baking mat, rolling pin, cookie sheet or jelly roll pan, medium bowl, small bowl, silicone spatula, pastry brush, fork

CRUST

1 cup (125g) all-purpose flour, plus extra for sprinkling on the dough and parchment

⅓ cup (25g) dark unsweetened cocoa

3 tablespoons sugar

¼ teaspoon salt

7 tablespoons (105ml) coconut oil, measured, and then frozen for about 20 minutes, until hard

1 large egg, plus 1 large egg white for glaze

3 tablespoons ice water, divided

FILLING

3 cups fresh fruit: berries, plums, peaches, or apricots, cut into ½-inch (12-mm) pieces, or peeled and thinly sliced pears

3 tablespoons, plus 1 teaspoon sugar

2 teaspoons cornstarch

Confectioners' sugar, to sprinkle on top, optional

• To make the dough, place the flour, cocoa, sugar, and salt into the bowl of a food processor. Pulse to mix. Cut the frozen coconut oil into pieces and add them to the bowl of the food processor. Pulse them into the flour mixture 10 times or cut the frozen oil pieces into the dry ingredients by hand, using two knives or a pastry cutter.

• Add the egg and 1 tablespoon (15ml) of the ice water to the bowl of the food processor. Pulse the mixture 5 times or mix it gently by hand. Add another tablespoon of the ice water and pulse the mixture another 5 times or mix it again gently by hand. Add the last tablespoon of water, pulsing or lightly mixing the dough for 10 to 15 seconds, until it looks like clumps of couscous; the dough does not have to come completely together.

• Cut off a large piece of plastic wrap, place the dough on top of it, lift the sides of the plastic to wrap it around the dough, and then flatten it into an 8-inch (20-cm) pancake. Place the dough in the freezer for 15 to 20 minutes, until it feels firm, but you can still press into it a little.

• Preheat the oven to 425°F (220°C) and place a rack in the lowest position in your oven.

• Cut off a large piece of parchment paper and sprinkle it with some all-purpose flour. Remove the dough from the plastic wrap and place it on top of the parchment. Sprinkle some flour on the dough and then place a second piece of parchment on top. Using a rolling pin, roll over the top of the parchment to smooth out the dough into a 12- to 13-inch (30- to 33-cm) round shape. Peel back the top piece of parchment paper and sprinkle some more flour over the dough, once or twice, while you are rolling. Place the parchment and rolled crust onto the cookie sheet or jelly roll pan.

• To make the filling, place the fruit in a medium bowl. In a small bowl, mix together the sugar and cornstarch, then sprinkle it on top of the fruit and mix it in gently until the flour dissolves. Place the fruit in the center of the dough circle and spread it outward, leaving a 2- to 3-inch (5- to 7.5-cm) border. Fold about 2 inches (5cm) of the border over the fruit, leaving the fruit-filled center open. Fold over another 2-inch (5-cm) section of the border and repeat this step, pressing one section of the border into the next, so that you end up with dough pleats all the way around. This will seal in the fruit (and fruit juices). Use a pastry brush to dust off any excess flour on the dough.

• Beat the reserved egg white with a fork, then brush the egg white all over the dough. Sprinkle it with the remaining teaspoon of sugar if you like. Bake for 30 minutes, then remove the pan from the oven. Using oven mitts, move the rack to the middle position, then move the galette back to the rack and bake for another 5 to 10 minutes or until filling looks bubbly. Let cool for 20 minutes and serve, dusted with confecitoners' sugar, if desired.

Dark Cocoa

Dark cocoa is a favorite recent ingredient that gives chocolate desserts deeper flavor and color. Whenever I substitute dark cocoa for the regular cocoa in a recipe, I add 2 tablespoons of sugar to the recipe to balance the slight bitterness of the dark cocoa.

GLUTEN-FREE CHALLAH

Parve, Gluten-free • Makes 1 large loaf

I probably receive a message or email every week from someone asking if I have a good gluten-free challah recipe. I finally have a recipe that is good enough to publish, thanks to Orly's gluten-free flour blends, which you can buy in stores and online. I use Orly's Manhattan mix. You can also use your favorite gluten-free flour mix. I tried braiding this recipe or making it into a round shape but was never satisfied with the result, so I highly recommend the silicone challah molds you can purchase online. This recipe was inspired by Orly's recipe.

PREP TIME: 15 minutes; 1½ hours for first rising; 45 minutes for second rising • BAKE TIME: 30 minutes • ADVANCE PREP: May be made 2 days in advance or frozen • EQUIPMENT: Measuring cups and spoons, silicone spatula or wooden spoon, mixing bowl, whisk, pastry brush, 1 silicone challah mold, jelly roll pan, or cookie sheet

2 envelopes (½ ounce [15g]) active dry yeast

⅓ cup (80ml) warm water

¼ cup (50g) plus 1 teaspoon sugar, divided

⅓ cup (80ml) plus 1 teaspoon sunflower or safflower oil, divided

⅓ cup (80ml) honey

2 teaspoons salt

½ cup (120ml) boiling water

¼ cup (60ml) cold water

2 large eggs, beaten

½ cup (45g) gluten-free oats

3½ to 4 cups (440 to 500g) gluten-free flour mix

Cooking spray for greasing pan

• In a measuring cup, dissolve the yeast in the warm water. Add 1 teaspoon of the sugar and mix it in. Let the mixture sit for 8 to 10 minutes, or until it is thick.

• In a large bowl, whisk together the oil, remaining ¼ cup (50g) sugar, honey, and salt. To dissolve them, whisk in the boiling water. Add the cold water and mix again. Beat the eggs in a separate bowl and add them to the oil mixture, reserving 2 to 3 teaspoons to brush on the loaves before baking. When the yeast bubbles, add the yeast mixture to the bowl and whisk.

• Add the oats and 1 cup (125g) of flour and whisk well. Add another cup (125g) of flour and mix well. Add a third cup (125g) of flour and mix. Add ½ cup (65g) of flour and knead it in. Turn out the dough onto the counter and add more flour and knead gently until the dough is mostly soft. Place the remaining teaspoon of oil into the bowl and rub it all around the bowl and on top of the dough. Place the dough in the oiled bowl and cover the bowl with plastic wrap. Let the dough rise for 1½ hours.

• Use cooking spray to grease the challah mold. Shape the challah into an oblong piece and then place into the mold. Let the dough rise for 45 minutes.

• Preheat the oven to 375°F (190°C). Bake the challah for 30 minutes. Remove it from the mold onto a cookie sheet or jelly roll pan. Add a teaspoon of water to the reserved egg and brush it over the challah. Bake it for another 10 minutes or until it is golden brown.

WHOLE-WHEAT ONION CHALLAH

Parve • Makes 2 medium loaves

Many of us New Yorkers remember Ratner's restaurant on the Lower East Side of Manhattan. Among their many specialties were onion rolls, light white-flour square rolls studded with chopped onions inside and out. My friend Miriam Alon, whose family first took me there, and I could not eat them fast enough. The best part about baking this onion challah is the aroma that will fill your kitchen—I imagine it to be just like what you might smell at Ratner's, or in a village bakery in Eastern Europe.

PREP TIME: 15 minutes; first rise 2 hours, 15 minutes to shape, second rise 1 hour • BAKE TIME: 30 minutes • ADVANCE PREP: May be made 3 days in advance or frozen • EQUIPMENT: Measuring cups and spoons, cutting board, knife, large bowl, whisk, 2 small bowls, medium bowl, wooden spoon or silicone spatula, stand mixer with dough hook attachment, plastic scraper, plastic wrap, cookie sheet or jelly roll pan, parchment or silicone baking mat, pastry brush

DOUGH

½ ounce [15g]) active dry yeast

⅓ cup (80ml) warm water

½ cup (100g) plus 2 teaspoons sugar, divided

½ cup (120ml) safflower, sunflower, or canola oil, plus 1 teaspoon for greasing the bowl

2 teaspoons salt

1 tablespoon honey

½ cup (120ml) boiling water

¼ cup (60ml) cold water

1½ cups (190g) white whole-wheat flour plus extra for dusting work surface

1¼ cups (130g) whole-wheat flour

1 cup (110g) spelt flour

3 large eggs, divided

FILLING

2 small onions, chopped into ¼-inch (6-mm) pieces (about 1 cup)

1 tablespoon poppy seeds

2 teaspoons caraway seeds

½ teaspoon salt

2 tablespoons safflower, sunflower, or canola oil

• Dissolve the yeast in the warm water and mix in 2 teaspoons of the sugar. Let the mixture sit for 10 minutes, or until it is thick.

• In a large bowl, whisk together the oil, salt, honey, and the remaining ½ cup (100g) of sugar. Add the boiling water to the bowl and whisk the mixture to dissolve the sugar and salt. Add the cold water and whisk it in. In a medium bowl, whisk together the white whole-wheat flour, whole-wheat flour, and spelt flour.

• Beat 2 eggs in a small bowl and add them to the oil mixture. Add the yeast mixture to the egg-and-oil mixture and whisk it well. Add 1 cup (120g) of the flour and whisk it into the liquids. Add another cup (120g) of the flour and use a wooden spoon or silicone spatula to mix it in. (You can also put the ingredients into the bowl of a stand mixer and mix with the dough hook attachment.) Add another cup (120g) of the flour and mix it in. Add ½ cup (60g) of flour and knead it into the dough until it's mostly smooth. If extremely sticky, add the final ¼ cup flour. It can be a little sticky.

• Sprinkle a counter with ½ tablespoon white whole-wheat flour. Remove the dough from the bowl and place on the dusted counter. To get all of the dough out, scrape the sides of the bowl with your fingers or a plastic scraper and gather the dough into a ball.

• Sprinkle another ½ tablespoon flour on top of the dough. Add 1 teaspoon of oil to the bowl and rub it around. Return the dough to the bowl, rub some oil on top of it, and cover the bowl with plastic wrap. Let the dough rise for 2 hours.

• While the dough is rising, place the chopped onions, poppy seeds, caraway seeds, salt, and oil into a small bowl and mix well. Cover the bowl with plastic wrap and set it aside until the dough has risen for 2 hours.

• Divide the dough in half, and sprinkle some white whole-wheat flour on top of the counter.

• Divide each half of the dough into three pieces. Roll each piece into a long strand, about 10 inches (25cm) long. Use your hands to flatten the strands and stretch them so that each is about 2½ to 3 inches (6 to 7.5cm) wide. Using the side of your hand, make a trough in the center of the dough lengthwise. Scoop up a heaping tablespoon of onion mixture and spread it along the center of the dough, into the indentation you've just made. Fold the dough over the filling and seal it, creating a long rope. Set it aside, with the seam on the bottom, while you prepare 2 other strands.

• When all 3 strands are filled, braid them together, tuck the ends underneath, and place the loaf on the cookie sheet or jelly roll pan covered with parchment or a silicone baking mat. Repeat the same steps for the second half of the dough and place the second loaf next to the first loaf, leaving a few inches (5 to 7.5cm) between them.

• Let the loaves rise for 1 hour.

• Preheat the oven to 350°F (180°C). Beat the remaining egg with 1 teaspoon of water in a small bowl, then brush the top and sides of the loaves. Sprinkle the remaining onion mixture on top of the loaves. Bake them for 30 minutes, or until the loaves are golden.

Baking with Yeast

Most recipes that use yeast instruct the baker to mix the yeast and a little sugar into warm water and let that sit until it thickens. I always use the hottest tap water, which cools a little by the time I add the yeast and sugar. If the mixture does not bubble after 10 minutes, then the yeast is dead. If that happens to you, dump out the mixture, rinse the bowl or measuring cup, and start again.

Baking Challah in Advance

I often bake challahs early in the week, as I have so many dishes to prepare on Friday for Shabbat. I fully bake my challahs, but I don't overbake them. After they have cooled completely, I wrap the challahs in heavy-duty aluminum foil and freeze them. A few hours before serving the loaves, I remove them from the freezer to thaw, then place them (still wrapped in foil) into a 300°F to 325°F (150°C to 160°C) oven for at least 25 minutes to warm them until they are pretty hot. Unwrap the challahs and serve them—they will taste like you just baked them.

ROSEMARY FOCACCIA

Parve, Vegan • Makes 1 12 x 16-inch (30 x 40-cm) flatbread (at least 12 servings)

When my family lived in Geneva, Switzerland, in the 1990s, we spent summers in the Tuscan beach town of Forte dei Marmi. Our favorite things to eat there were panini made from focaccia and filled with different vegetables and cheeses. They are called "focaccina," and, when I returned to Forte in 2016, I learned that the sandwiches are still as great as ever. I enjoyed one with porcini mushrooms and a cream cheese–like spread. Here is a recipe for focaccia that is very easy to make. You can cut it into strips to serve with soup or as a different bread for Shabbat lunch, or cut it into squares for sandwiches. After the first day, I always toast my slices.

PREP TIME: 10 minutes; first rise 1 hour, second rise 2 hours • BAKE TIME: 25 minutes • ADVANCE PREP: May be made 3 days in advance or frozen • EQUIPMENT: Measuring cups and spoons, stand mixer with dough hook attachment, plastic wrap, jelly roll pan, wooden spoon, cutting board. knife

BREAD

3 cups (375g) plus 3 tablespoons (25g) all-purpose flour, divided

4 cups (520g) whole-wheat flour

3½ cups (840g) warm water

1½ teaspoons yeast

1 tablespoon kosher salt

Extra virgin olive oil for greasing bowl

TOPPING

⅓ cup (80ml) plus 2 tablespoons (30ml) extra virgin olive oil, divided, plus extra for greasing bowl

¼ teaspoon kosher salt

2 teaspoons finely chopped fresh rosemary

• Place 3 cups of the all-purpose flour, whole-wheat flour, water, and yeast in the bowl of a stand mixer with a dough hook attachment and combine, then continue for 1 minute more, or mix by hand. The mixture will be sticky. Cover the bowl with plastic wrap and let the dough rise for 1 hour.

• Add the salt to the dough, and mix with the hook attachment for 5 minutes. Place 1 tablespoon (7.5g) of all-purpose flour on the counter. Turn the dough

out onto the counter and coat both sides with the flour. Knead the dough a few times, adding 1 or 2 tablespoons (7.5g to 15g) of flour if the dough is very sticky. Grease the bowl with a little oil and place the dough back into the bowl. Cover it with plastic wrap and let the dough rise for another hour.

• Place ⅓ cup (80ml) of the olive oil on a jelly roll pan (the pan you use must have sides). Place the dough on top and press and stretch it toward the corners of the pan as best as you can, without getting oil on yourself. Cover the pan loosely with plastic wrap and let the dough rise for 10 minutes. Every few minutes, press on top of the plastic wrap to stretch the dough into the corners, without causing the oil to tsunami over the sides of the pan, and lift the plastic so it does not stick to the dough. Preheat the oven to 450°F (230°C).

• Remove the plastic wrap and use the end of a wooden spoon to poke holes in the dough, about every 2 inches (5cm). Drizzle the remaining 2 tablespoons (30ml) of olive oil on top of the dough. Sprinkle it with kosher salt and chopped rosemary. Bake the bread for 25 minutes. As soon as it is cool enough to handle, slice it, and start eating.

SOURDOUGH CHALLAH

Parve, Vegetarian • Makes 2 medium loaves

I know what you're thinking: "Huh? Why would anyone want that?" So I'm here to share the gospel of Michael Pollan, who, in his wonderful documentary series *Cooked*, talks about how, for centuries, people ate bread every day and were not obese and pre-diabetic. He explains that the bread people ate was made from starters, not commercial yeast, and people were healthier. Once the American food industry starting producing commercial yeast and commercial bread, people began getting fat and sick. Rather than reconsider the introduction of commercial yeast to bread production and return to the old-fashioned method, companies found ways to fortify packaged breads. Americans still got fat and sick. In areas of the world where people live to be over 100 years old and who are not fat and sick, they eat locally made bread that is baked daily. So we don't get sick and fat from eating bread, we get sick and fat from eating the *wrong* bread.

We need the bacteria in bread made from sourdough starter for gut health. I started making sourdough to make sandwich bread for my kids, and then decided to try a sourdough challah. It took many tries, and you will see that it takes 2 days to make this recipe, although the amount of actual effort is minimal. Here is a partially whole-wheat sourdough challah—a challah you can feel good about eating—thanks to Josey Baker, a master bread baker in San Francisco, whose bread inspired me to start baking sourdough in 2015, and whose book, *Josey Baker Bread* (Chronicle, 2014), taught me the basics of the process. I was not happy with the look of this dough when it was braided by hand, so I bake it in silicone molds that look like braided challahs.

PREP TIME: Starter sits for 2 weeks before first use; preferment sits 12 hours to 2 days; 5 minutes, plus 12 hours to chill • COOK TIME: 35 to 40 minutes • ADVANCE PREP: May be made 2 days in advance or frozen • EQUIPMENT: Measuring cups and spoons, medium jar or bowl, plastic wrap, silicone spatula or wooden spoon, 2 large bowls, small bowl, whisk, 2 silicone challah molds, cookie sheet or jelly roll pan, pastry brush

STARTER

3½ to 4 cups (840 to 960ml) water, divided

3½ to 4 cups (455 to 520mg) whole-wheat flour, divided

PREFERMENT*

1 cup (240ml) warm water

1 cup (130g) whole-wheat flour bread flour

¼ cup starter

DOUGH

¾ cup (150g) sugar

1 tablespoon salt

½ cup (120ml) safflower, sunflower, or canola oil

½ cup (120ml) boiling water

¼ cup (60ml) cold water

3 large eggs

4½ to 5 cups (565 to 625g) bread flour

Cooking spray for greasing pan

• To make the starter, combine ½ cup water and ½ cup whole-wheat flour in a medium jar or bowl and mix well. Cover the mixture with plastic wrap and let it sit at room temperature for 2 days. Dump out most of the mixture, leaving only about a tablespoon in the jar or bowl. Feed the starter by adding ½ cup (120ml) of cool water and another ½ cup (65g) of whole-wheat flour and mix it well. Let the mixture sit for another 2 to 3 days. Repeat this process for 2 weeks total; when you open the jar or bowl, the mixture should give off a sour smell. I like to feed the starter 12 hours before I use it to make bread. After 2 weeks you can keep the starter in the fridge and do the dumping and feeding every few weeks. After you feed it, let the starter sit out at room temperature for a few hours before you return it to the fridge.

• To make the preferment for your dough, place the warm water, the bread flour, and ¼ cup (53g) of the starter in a large bowl and mix it well. Cover the bowl with plastic wrap and let it sit for at least 12 hours and up to 2 days. I like to mix the preferment in the evening and let it sit until the next evening. (You can save the remaining starter for another loaf, just continue to feed every few days and store in the fridge.)

• To make the dough, place the sugar, salt, and oil in a large bowl. Add the boiling water and whisk well. Add the cold water and mix again. Beat the eggs in a small bowl and add them to the large bowl, reserving 1 tablespoon to brush on the loaves before baking. Whisk well. Add 3 cups (375g) of the bread flour, 1 cup at a time, mixing well after the addition of each cup. Add the preferment mixture and mix well. Add another cup (125g) of flour and mix it in. Turn out the dough onto the counter and mix it with your hands. Add ½ cup (65g) of flour and mix it into the dough. If the dough is still sticky, add another ¼ cup (30g) of flour and mix it in, until the dough is mostly smooth and flour is totally mixed in. There is no need to do much kneading, just mix in the flour. Cover the bowl with plastic wrap and set aside.

• After 30 minutes, uncover the bowl, dip your hand in water, lift up part of the dough, and fold it into the center of the ball of dough. Turn the bowl and fold over another section of the dough. Continue until you have made your way all around the ball of dough. Cover the bowl again and let sit for another 30 minutes. Repeat the folding process and let the dough sit for another 30 minutes. Repeat the process for 2 more cycles, for a total of 2½ hours of sitting.

• Cover the bowl with fresh plastic wrap and let the dough sit and rise for 12 hours.

• Sprinkle some bread flour on your counter and hands. Divide the dough into 2 pieces and knead each gently for 1 minute and shape it into an oval if you're going to use challah molds. Grease the mold with cooking spray, and then place the dough in the mold. Let rise for 1 hour.

• Preheat the oven to 350°F (180°C). Place the molds (dough facing up) directly on the middle oven rack and bake for 20 minutes. Meanwhile, in a small bowl add 1 teaspoon of water to the reserved egg and mix well. Set it aside.

• After 20 minutes, remove the molds from the oven and turn the challahs onto a jelly roll pan covered with parchment paper or a silicone mat. Brush the top of the challahs with the egg wash. Bake them for another 15 to 20 minutes, or until they are well browned.

Preferment

A preferment is a preparation of a portion of a bread dough that is made several hours or more in advance of mixing the final dough.

Timeline

• Make your starter, knowing that in 2 weeks you can make this recipe and other sourdough breads.
• Make your preferment between 6 and 8 pm one night (on Wednesday, if you want the bread for Shabbat).
• Mix the dough between 6 and 8 pm the next night. You can then do the folding and let the dough sit overnight (Thursday night).
• Bake the loaves on Friday, in the late morning.

About the Author

Paula Shoyer, known as "the kosher baker," is the author of *The Holiday Kosher Baker*, *The Kosher Baker: 160 dairy-free recipes* and *The New Passover Menu*. She is a freelance writer for the *Washington Post*, *Hadassah*, *Joy of Kosher*, and *Jewish Food Experience*. Paula graduated from the Ritz Escoffier in Paris and teaches cooking and baking across the United States and around the world for Jewish organizations, synagogues, book festivals, and more.

Paula competed on Food Network's *Sweet Genius* and appeared on TV before Jewish holidays on shows such as *Home & Family* on Hallmark Channel, Fox News New York, San Diego Living, and the local Washington, D.C., stations—over 26 appearances. In 2015, Paula was honored by Jewish Women International as a "Woman to Watch" and in 2016 as a "kosher food pioneer" by the kosher food bloggers community. Paula edited the popular cookbooks *Kosher by Design Entertains* and *Kosher by Design Kids in the Kitchen* (both from Mesorah Publications). She lives in Chevy Chase, Maryland, with her husband and four children. To learn more about Paula Shoyer, visit thekosherbaker.com.

You can find her at www.thekosherbaker.com
Instagram: **kosherbaker**
Facebook: **Paula Shoyer; The Kosher Baker**
Twitter: **Paula Shoyer**

Acknowledgments

I am so blessed to have such a wonderful family. Husband Andy and children Emily, Sam, Jake, and Joey are the front line in my recipe development. Thank you all for encouraging me to get off the sofa and write a new cookbook. I am successful because each of you loves me, cheers me on and promotes me, is honest about the recipes, and takes care of yourself when I am on the road. Jake, thank you for allowing me to bake without margarine and for agreeing to eat whole-grain desserts; I know it's a huge sacrifice.

Thank you to all my cheerleaders: Reubin Marcus, z"l, my late father, who got to taste many of these recipes when he moved to Maryland in November 2016, my mother-law-law, Lillian Shoyer, brothers Adam and Ezra Marcus, and Ezra's wife, Tamar, and niece and nephew, Naomi and Yonatan, brother-in-law Steve Shoyer and wife, Debbie Horwitz, and niece and nephew, Claire and Ben.

Hugs to Limor Decter, my personal Yoda, Oprah, and Sherpa, who guides me through every step of every book. Thanks to the additional, non-recipe-testing team members, who listen and support, through all my successes and painful losses these past two-plus years: Judith Gold, Karina Schumer, Amanda Goldstein, Pamela Auerbach, Robyn Lieberman, Lily Starr, Laurie Strongin, Pam Shrock, Tammy Landy, Aron and Elisha Freidman, Kathy Ingber, Lisa Weitzman, and Brian Israel.

Thank you to Betty Supo for the expert cooking advice, inspiration in the kitchen, and all the help you provide every day.

I am so thankful for my expert team of recipe testers who keep coming back for more: Debbie, Steve, Claire and Ben Shoyer, Elena Lefkowitz, Melissa and Mark Arking, Marla and Andrew Satinsky, Esther Dayon, Trudy Jacobson, Shira Broms, Donna Meltzer and Andrea Neusner, team gluten-free expert. Thanks to nutritionist Jessica Grosman, who kept inspiring me to go healthier and healthier.

After three books together, the people at Sterling Publishing are practically family. President Theresa Thompson has been my biggest supporter and advocate of my projects. My senior editor and friend Jennifer Williams makes everything go smoothly because she truly appreciates my vision for my books. Gratitude to my fabulous project editor Hannah Reich, who is both caring and competent; thank you for our little battles within Track Changes that result in a better book. Thank you to Betsy Beier, editorial director, Elizabeth Lindy, jacket art director, Jo Obarowski, creative director, Chris Bain, photo director, and Shannon Plunkett, interior designer, the team I lived with for four days during the photo shoot in New York and who also helped me air-traffic-control my children when needed. This book, from concept to final edits and everything in between, was a lifeline to me over the past difficult year and a half; together, everyone at Sterling gave me a great gift.

Kudos to photographer Bill Milne, whose talent and charm won me over instantly. You were able to make real the photography concept I had in my head.

Thank you once again to my agent Sally Ekus of The Lisa Ekus Group, who believes in me and my work. Look what we have accomplished together in just five years!

Resources

www.thepeppermill.com
kosher baking ingredients, cooking equipment

www.amazon.com
cooking and baking equipment
kosher gochujang paste

www.thekoshercook.com
silicone challah molds

www.spicejungle.com
kosher certified unusual spices including ras el hanout and Aleppo pepper

Index